Full *of* Grace

Full *of* Grace

Women and the Abundant Life

Johnnette S. Benkovic

CHARIS

SERVANT PUBLICATIONS
ANN ARBOR, MICHIGAN

Charis Books is an imprint of Servant Publications especially designed to serve Roman Catholics.

Unless otherwise noted, all Scripture quotations in this book are from the *Revised Standard Version,* © 1946, 1952, 1957, 1965, 1966, by the Division of Christian Education of the National Council of the Churches of Christ in the United States of America. Published by Thomas Nelson Publishers for Ignatius Press. Used by permission. Scripture quotations also taken from *The New American Bible, St. Joseph Edition,* © 1970 The Old Testament and © 1986 Revised New Testament. © 1992, 1987, 1980, 1970 by Catholic Book Publishing Co., New York, N.Y.; *New Revised Standard Version,* © 1989 by the Division of Christian Education of the National Council of the Churches of Christ in the United States of America. Published by Thomas Nelson Publishers, Inc., Nashville, Tenn.; *Douay-Rheims Version,* reprinted by TAN Books and Publishers, Inc., Rockford, Ill.

Excerpts from the English translation of the *Catechism of the Catholic Church* for the United States of America, © 1994, United States Catholic Conference, Inc. – Libreria Editrice Vaticana. Used by permission.

Excerpts from *Three Ages of the Interior Life* by Fr. Garrigou-Lagrange, O.P., were used by permission of the publisher, TAN Books and Publishers, Inc. All rights reserved.

Excerpts from *In Conversation with God* by Francis Fernandez and from various works of Blessed Josemaría Escrivá were used by permission of Scepter Publications. All rights reserved.

Published by Servant Publications
P.O. Box 8617
Ann Arbor, Michigan 48107

98 99 00 01 10 9 8 7 6 5 4 3 2 1

Printed in the United States of America
ISBN 0-89283-960-0

LIBRARY OF CONGRESS CATALOGING-IN-PUBLICATION DATA

Benkovic, Johnnette S.
Full of grace : women and the abundant life / Johnnette S. Benkovic.
    p.   cm.
Includes bibliographical references.
ISBN 0-89283-960-0 (alk. paper)
1. Catholic women—Religious life.   2. Women (Christian theology)   I. Title.
BX2353.B45   1998
248.8'43—dc21   97-45997
                                                                     CIP

I lovingly dedicate this book to my husband,
Anthony,
whose unwavering support
and constant understanding
gave me the
freedom, courage, and faith
to write it.

Contents

The Special Call and Gift of Woman

*S*he was a humble maiden, young in years but wise in the ways of God. The days of her youth had been filled with prayer, anticipation, and faithful adherence to the Law of Moses. Mary (or "Miriam," as she was called in Hebrew) knew that the Messiah would come. Though the time of His coming was a mystery, she waited with patience and expectant faith, performing the common duties of her station, eager for the fulfillment of the prophets' words.

During those days of hopeful anticipation, as she went about saying her prayers, praising God, caring for that which was entrusted to her, she couldn't have known that she would figure so profoundly in the fulfillment of the Messianic prophecy. Couldn't have known that she had been specifically chosen by God the Father to be *Theotokos*, the "God-bearer," the one whose womb would be filled with the Word of God. Couldn't have known that, because of her "yes" to God, the gates of heaven would be thrown open through the gift of redemptive grace.

It must have been like any other day, that particular day when the fullness of time had arrived. Perhaps rain streamed from the skies like so many bands of gray ribbon. Or perhaps the sun shone with a fierce intensity that penetrated the cold layers of mankind's heart. In the midst of that ordinary day the brilliance of heaven lit the sky and an angelic being stood before her.

"Full of Grace," he called her. "Blessed are you among women. Behold, you will conceive in your womb and bear a son, and you shall call His name Jesus. He will be great, and will be called the Son of the Most High; and the Lord God will give to him the throne of his father David, and he will reign over the house of Jacob forever, and of his kingdom there will be no end.... The Holy Spirit will come upon you, and the power of the Most High will overshadow you; therefore the child to be born will be called holy, the Son of God" (Lk 1:31-33, 35).

And so, this humble woman-child came to know that she was the one chosen by God from all eternity to bear redemption to the world. The early Church Fathers tell us that all of heaven held its breath, waiting for her answer, for the salvation of the world depended upon it. With what gratitude and relief did heaven sigh when the Virgin Mary said, "I am the handmaid of the Lord; be it done unto me according to your word" (Lk 1:38). Her "yes," proclaimed in humble submission to the will of the Father, allowed redemptive grace to enter the world and alter the destiny of mankind.

Called by God to Bring Salvation to the World

We know that, at the moment of the Annunciation, the Blessed Virgin Mary was uniquely commissioned to bring Jesus into the world. She was to become the perfect channel of God's greatest Gift. This is why we esteem her above all the saints, for God entrusted this singular and holy honor to Mary alone.

And yet, in a certain sense, God extends the call He issued to Mary to each of us. *Will you bring my Son into the world? Will you carry Him in the womb of your heart as Mary carried Him in the womb of her body? Will you birth Him into the lives of others, that all might come to experience the grace of redemption and eternal life?*

Like the Blessed Mother, you and I have a choice. We can say "yes" to God's request, or we can say "no." And, just like Mary's response, our answer has eternal consequences, both in our lives and in the lives of others. If we say "yes" as Mary did, God will empower us with His Holy Spirit and we, too, will be filled with the life of Jesus Christ. Like Mary, we will become a channel of grace through which the love of God enters into the world. And, because the spiritual needs of our day are so great, all of heaven is holding its breath waiting for our response.

Mary, Our Mother of Grace

Because Mary was the woman God selected from all time to give birth to His Son, Jesus Christ, she figured prominently in the redemption of the human race. Her role in salvation history began with the conception of Jesus and it continues throughout time. The Fathers of the Second Vatican Council tell us, "In a wholly singular way she [Mary] cooperated by her obedience, faith, hope, and burning charity in the work of the Savior in restoring supernatural life to souls. For this reason she is mother to us in the order of grace."[1] Just as Mary gave birth to Jesus Christ through her womb, so she continues to bring spiritual life to the people of God through her Immaculate Heart. She is the "Mother of grace" for God's children.

In contemporary times, one way we have seen the Blessed Virgin Mary bring spiritual life to God's people is through her many apparitions, which are being reported all over the world. While most of them are still under investigation by the Roman Catholic Church, others have received full approval. In many of these appearances, Mary informs us about our life in God, instructs us how to live God-centered lives, and inspires us to proceed along the path of righteousness. In other cases, the Blessed Mother is silent or weeping or praying. In all cases, she comes as a mother who longs to give spiritual life to her children by leading them to her Son, Jesus Christ, the Savior of the World.

The number of these appearances tells us how spiritually desperate are the times in which we live. So spiritually corrupt is the world that God is sending the mother of His Son around the globe as a signpost leading us to the path of truth. How much He must love us! Because Mary points us to her Son, her appearances are a special outpouring of mercy alerting us that NOW is the time to accept redemptive grace. And because she is woman and mother, Mary's coming suggests that in these days women who follow her example will join her in dispensing the mercy of God to His children by leading them to the One who is Salvation, Jesus Christ.

The Time for Woman Is Now

In their closing message of the Second Vatican Council, the Council Fathers expressed an urgent plea for women to accept God's call:

The hour is coming, in fact has come, when the vocation of woman is being acknowledged in its fullness, the hour in which women acquire in the world an influence, an effect and a power never hitherto achieved. That is why, at this moment when the human race is undergoing so deep a transformation, women impregnated with a spirit of the Gospel can do so much to aid humanity in not falling.[2]

This appeal of the Council Fathers leads us to ask the following three questions:

1. *What is the vocation of woman?*
2. *What should be the influence of woman's vocation in the world?*
3. *What does it mean to be impregnated with the spirit of the gospel?*

Discovering the answers to these questions will show us how women have been especially graced by God to meet the challenge of today's world *"to aid humanity in not falling."*

What Is the Vocation of Woman?

God has uniquely created woman to share in His most sovereign act—the bringing of life.

A Lesson From Nature

As I write these words, rain is falling from the heavens outside of my window. Though its humble action seems so commonplace as to be almost insignificant, this soft rain is a catalyst for the mysterious unfolding of life.

The rhythmic beat of the raindrops speaks of life beyond what our human vision reveals, a reality beyond what our finite minds can capture, a truth deep and mysterious but available to all. That gentle cadence is but a herald of all that is seen and unseen, of the life we know and the life we have yet to discover.

As the soil surrenders to the rainwater's caress, it mingles with it, assimilates it, becomes one with it. No longer hard and cold, the earth's rough exterior is softened, giving way to something more, something laden with possibilities. In mutual self-donation, rain and soil yield to nature's fertile potential.

Like tendrils of life, rivulets of water flow through the soil to the seed lying hidden just beneath the earth's surface. The seed's crusty coat is drenched in a moisturizing bath; it absorbs the water and the seed's interior tissue swells. At the appointed time, the seed coat bursts and new life sinks itself into the soil. The soil's properties nourish the tender shoot until, at long last, the tiny life pokes through the ground and what was once unseen emerges into the light of day. Rain, soil, and seed—symbols of life, from real life, about real life.

Woman's Life-Bearing Potential

As women, we are called to real life. But just as the seed lies hidden beneath the surface of the soil, so our real life is often shrouded and unseen. Buried deep within the confines of our inner being, our life-bearing potential needs the gentle rain of grace and the soft rich soil of truth to grow and flourish. As we surrender to the soaking presence of God's grace active within us, like the rain, the gift of our womanhood brings not only physical life, but spiritual life as well. This is the call of woman: *to infuse all the world with life.*

What Should Be the Influence of Woman's Vocation?

Everything about woman has been created by God to bring life. From the delicate intricacy of the female body to the complex artistry of our emotional makeup, women have been chosen by God to participate in His exquisite and sovereign act of bringing, nurturing, and sustaining life.

We see this so clearly in the magnificent composition of the female body. Just as the illustration from nature shows the harmonious effort of seed, soil, and rain in the bringing of life, the individual components of the female body function with graceful precision to produce life.

The Miracle of Physical Motherhood

With an accuracy that inspires wonder, female hormones direct the life-producing process. Once the ovaries release the egg, tiny as a pencil-point, its journey to life begins. Egg and sperm meet in mutual self-donation, giving way to something more—a new life, chosen by God.

The womb gives itself over to the new life, growing and expanding as the child within it grows and expands. And at the appointed time, the womb begins to contract, slowly and insistently at first, but steadily quickening and intensifying, until, in an explosive moment of agony and ecstasy, the baby is born. God chose to contain within the female body the entire spectrum of humanity. In the ovaries of woman have resided the origins of all the generations of mankind will ever have life. Thus, in the microcosm of the female body lies the whole of created human reality.[3] Though man participates in the creative process, he is but a channel through which the possibility of life passes. It is within woman that the seed of life germinates, roots, and grows. In an act of self-donation, a woman gives her whole person for the benefit of the other growing within her. First, she gives her body to be the safe haven which houses the new life. She will experience its changing appearance, its physical expansion, its interior reorganization. Flesh will stretch; inner organs will move; tissues will swell as her body accommodates itself to the new life growing within.

The woman gives her emotional composition, too. Riding the tide of changing hormones, she holds fast as the unpredictable ebb and flow pull her from nervous anticipation to giddy elation to peace-filled contentment to unexplainable sorrow.

In the midst of all the physical and emotional change, the woman gives still more. She gives her child the gift of love—a cord that binds mother to child more intimately than any physical connection could ever unite them. Everything the woman chooses to do is seen in light of this love. Her diet, activities, and schedules may change. Her priorities shift. Her plans, present and future, are reconsidered. She concerns herself for the child's well-being and health, for the child's birth and future.

As time goes on the woman grows ever more involved with this child whom her body bears. She gets to know it, and know it well. She knows its habits, its baby ways. She knows when it is restless and when it is at peace. She talks to her child, cooing to her swollen belly in soothing words and songs. She prays for her child, invests hopes and dreams in it, asks for God's guidance in raising it and nurturing it to full maturity.

She loves the baby completely and totally. She lives no longer for herself, an autonomous being, but rather for another, her child. Months before the baby is ever placed in her arms, the woman, who already has become mother, discovers that she is in a unique and special relationship with this child, her offspring, the fruit of her womb.

Woman's Physical Capacity Mirrors a Spiritual Reality

The *Catechism of the Catholic Church* states that "the human person, created in the image and likeness of God, is a being at once corporeal and spiritual" (#362). That is, we are comprised of a body and a soul. "In sacred Scripture the term 'soul' often refers to human *life* or the entire human *person*" (#363). It is "the real spiritual substance created by God,"[4] the innermost aspect of our human person, that which is of greatest value, for it is made in the image of God. Our soul is the very essence of who we are and who we can become. It is also immortal.

A profound unity exists between the soul and the body. They are not two separate natures joined together in the human person, but rather they are an integrated union that forms a single nature. So incorporated are the soul and body that the Council of Vienne (1311–12) declared our souls to be the "immediate substantial" form of our bodies. This means that our femininity is as inherent to our souls as it is to our bodies. Our gender defines us not only physically, but metaphysically as well.[5] We are woman completely— in body and soul. Thus, our gender reveals and defines the innermost aspect of who we are.

The Reality of Spiritual Motherhood

Because *"Everything in the feminine being* is dominated by the constitution which makes her capable of carrying and forming another being originating in her own," the spiritual reality of our femininity speaks to the very influence in the world that God intends for woman.

If the preeminent function of our womanly bodies is to bring life, as we have just discussed, the preeminent function of our womanly soul—our feminine spirit and psyche—must be to bring life as well. Our entire being is meant to be life-giving, life-producing. Our call to bring life to others, then, does not stop at the physical level, but only begins there.

By virtue of the gift of our gender, each of us is intended to be "mother." Just as our bodies have been created with the capacity to bear physical life, our souls have been especially created by God to bring *spiritual* life to the world. Thus, our call to motherhood is in no way diminished or negated by a life of celibacy or an inability to physically bear children. *All women are meant to bring life.*

Just as physical life roots and grows in the female body when sperm and egg meet, so spiritual life roots and grows within the feminine soul when the seed of faith is planted in the Sacrament of Baptism.

Just as our bodies are filled with new life when we conceive a child, so our souls are to be filled with the life of God. Just as the womb swells with the growth and development of our child, so the womb of our heart expands with the love and mercy of God. Just as new life issues forth from our bodies in an awesome moment of mystery and wonder, so our every word and deed should be a conduit of grace and new life for others.

And just as we love our child from the very depths of our being, so God's love should flow through us to the world as a soothing and healing balm. In this way our hearts and souls become conveyors of spiritual life.

Munus: Every Woman's Divine Call

Our holy call to spiritual motherhood might best be described by the Greek word *munus,* a word rich with intention.[7] Simply put, *munus* is a divine task, a divine duty or mission that God asks us to fulfill. Though there is accountability attached to the service, it is an honor to be asked to perform it.

Our feminine nature endows us with the attributes needed to fulfill our divine *munus* to bear spiritual life to the world. *"Woman naturally seeks to embrace that which is living, personal, and whole. To cherish, guard, protect, nourish and advance growth is her natural, maternal yearning."*[8] Everything about woman is ordered to this end. Her body, her psyche, and her soul equip her to be a nurturing influence in family life, in professional life, through her religious vocation, and in the world at large. Perhaps this is why our Council Fathers furthered their appeal to the women of the world in the closing speeches of the Second Vatican Council:

Reconcile men with life and above all, we beseech you, watch carefully over the future of our race. Hold back the hand of man, who, in a moment of folly, might attempt to destroy human civilization.... Women of the entire universe ... you to whom life is entrusted at this grave moment in history, it is for you to save the peace of the world.[9]

What Does It Mean to Be "Impregnated With the Spirit of the Gospel"?

The dictionary defines the word *impregnated* as "to be saturated with, permeated, pervaded." If we are to live out the call that God has in mind for us, we must be saturated with the gospel spirit, permeated with the gospel truth, and filled with the gospel life. Like the rain-soaked soil in our illustration, we must surrender and conform ourselves to Jesus Christ, the Seed of Life.

And yet, this process is not a simple one, for the way is fraught with unforeseen challenges and snares. Who, then, can show us the way? Who can lead us in our quest? Who can show us how to fulfill our mission?

The Blessed Mother: The Perfect Model of Womanhood
It is the Blessed Virgin Mary, the one who was filled with the very life of God, who best models for us how to live out the fullness of our feminine nature. It is she who shows us how to permeate our culture with the living Word of God. The Blessed Mother perfectly demonstrates both physical and spiritual motherhood.

We have only to look at the period of her maternity. What was it that took place within Mary during those nine months when she was with child? Joseph Cardinal Ratzinger refers to this stage of Mary's motherhood as her becoming "a field for the word."

*To be a field for the word means to be earth which allows itself to be absorbed by the seed, which assimilates itself to the seed, renouncing itself so as to make the seed germinate. With her motherhood Mary transfused into it her very substance, body and soul, so that a new life might come forth.... **Mary makes herself completely available as the soil, she allows herself to be used and consumed so as to be transformed into him.**[10]*

Mary renounced herself out of concern for the Child she carried, as mothers do, so that the life within her might germinate and come to full term. During her period of confinement, Mary made herself completely available to the Child developing within her, nurturing the tender life until it was time for Him to be born.

And yet, the totality of Mary's surrender must have been qualitatively different than the purely natural surrender of a mother to a child. She must have given herself to the Child in her womb with the same submission she gave to God at the moment of the Annunciation—for it was, in fact, God whom she carried within her. In response to the rain of God's grace that had prepared her to receive the God-man within her womb, Mary assimilated herself to the Seed of Life she carried, and was imbued with the Spirit of the Gospel.

For us to fulfill our call as spiritual mothers, we too must assimilate ourselves to Jesus Christ. In so doing, we will become a blessing to the world.

Mary Carries God's Blessing.

The Old Testament tradition teaches that when a person is blessed by God, that person carries God's blessings to others. That person's very presence becomes a source of healing, hope, and new life.

This is seen clearly at the moment of Mary's visitation to Elizabeth. St. Luke tells us that when Elizabeth hears Mary's voice, she proclaims, "Blessed are you among women, and blessed is the fruit of your womb. And why is this granted me, that the mother of my Lord should come to me? For behold, when the voice of your greeting came to my ears, the babe in my womb leaped for joy. And blessed is she who believed that there would be a fulfilment of what was spoken to her from the Lord" (Lk 1:42-45).

In her exhortation, Elizabeth confirmed the Angel Gabriel's words that Mary carried the blessing of God. Indeed, God Incarnate was enfleshed in Mary's womb. Note that Mary's greeting to Elizabeth is not recorded; it is Mary's presence that is the source of the blessing. Mary, imbued with the Word of God, radiated the presence of Jesus Christ.

Today Mary remains the very image of her Son, Jesus Christ, the Second Person of the Blessed Trinity. Wherever she is present, He is, too. She is always bringing her Son to others, and always bringing others to her Son. This is her *munus,* her divine call. She is the Spiritual Mother *par excellence,* always birthing Salvation to the world. Full of grace, Mary is impregnated with the Spirit of the Gospel and radiates that divine energy that initiates others into God's own life.

Like Mary, we are called to surrender to the life of God active within us through grace. We, too, must surrender to our Lord and Savior, become impregnated with the Spirit of the Gospel, and become conformed to His Image growing within the wombs of our hearts. We, too, must be full of grace so that the abundant life of Jesus Christ lives in us and through us. Thus will we fulfill our *munus* of spiritual motherhood and "do so much to aid humanity in not falling."

Called to Radiate the Life of Christ

People often tell my husband and me that they could point out our children in a crowd, so much do they resemble us. *As Christians, we should be that recognizable as the Father's children. Our very appearance should radiate His presence.* The words we speak, our attitudes, our actions should magnify His divine life within us.

We must stand out as lights in the darkness, become signs of God's love in a nation seduced by humanism and enchanted with lies. We must be purveyors of life in a culture infatuated with death. Bearing the life of God within us, we must offer love in the image of our Father to those who have not yet heard. This is our mission as woman. This is our call as spiritual mother. This is authentic femininity.

The Secret Beauty of Authentic Femininity

Writing in *Mother of the Redeemer,* Pope John Paul II says this about the call of woman in the world today:

> *The figure of Mary of Nazareth sheds light on womanhood as such by the very fact that God, in the sublime event of the Incarnation of his Son, entrusted himself to the ministry, the free and active ministry of a woman. **It can thus be said that women, by looking to Mary, find in her the secret of living their femininity with dignity and of achieving their own true advancement. In the light of Mary, the Church sees in the face of women the reflection of a beauty which mirrors the loftiest sentiments of which the human heart is capable:** the self-offering totality of love; the strength that is capable of bearing the greatest sorrows; limitless fidelity and tireless devotion to work; the ability to combine penetrating intuition with words of support and encouragement.*[11]

Writing more than sixty years earlier, Blessed Edith Stein says this about the feminine model presented by the life of the Blessed Virgin Mary:

> *Were we to present ... the image of the purely developed character of spouse and mother as it should be according to her natural vocation, we must gaze upon the Virgin Mary. In the center of her life stands her son. She awaits His birth in blissful expectation; she watches over His childhood; near or far, indeed, wherever He wishes, she follows Him on His way; she holds the crucified body in her arms; she carries out the will of the departed. But not as her action does she do all this: she is in this the Handmaid of the Lord; she fulfills that to which God has called her.*[12]

Once again Mary, our Spiritual Mother, shows us how to fulfill our call. If we are to be imbued with the Spirit of the Gospel and mirror "the loftiest sentiments of which the human heart is capable," Jesus Christ must stand in the center of our lives and we must be a handmaid of the Lord.

Handmaids of the Lord

A handmaid of the Lord is imbued with the love of God, is ready to serve God according to His will, and desires to awaken and nurture the Divine Life in others.[13] These characteristics and efforts come about not through the human efforts and good intentions of the handmaid, but through the gift of self-donation she makes to God, demonstrated by her complete cooperation with His divine initiative of grace.

There are three essential interior dispositions we must develop if, like the Virgin Mary, we are to be handmaids in the world today:

1. we must be **receptive** to the action of God;
2. we must **trust** in His never-failing providence in spite of circumstances; and
3. we must **surrender** to His holy will in all things.

In so doing, we will enter with true abandon into our call to bring life to the world and to "aid humanity in not falling." In his apostolic letter, *On the Dignity and Vocation of Women*, Pope John Paul II extols the vast numbers of holy women who have carried the torch of faith in apostolic service down through the ages:

> *In every age and in every country we find many "perfect" women who, despite persecution and discrimination, have shared in the Church's mission…. Even in the face of serious social discrimination, holy women have acted "freely," strengthened by their union with Christ. Such union and freedom rooted in God explain, for example, the great work of St. Catherine of Siena in the life of the Church, and the work of St. Teresa of Jesus in monastic life. In our own days too the Church is constantly enriched by the witness of the many women who fulfill their vocation to holiness. Holy women are an incarnation of the feminine ideal; they are also a model for all Christians, a model of the "sequela Christi," an example of how the Bride must respond with love to the love of the Bridegroom.*[14]

God has chosen for us to be the "perfect" women of our day and age. If we desire to fulfill the plan of God for us then we too must seek after holiness, and desire to be *"reclothed in Christ Jesus and refreshed by His Spirit."*[15] Our hearts must be set upon the higher things—upon holiness and truth, grace and obedience, commitment and love. Thus, full of grace, we will radiate the splendor of the Bridegroom's love to His people. Each facet of our being will become a prism of God's image alive within us, reflecting a holy aura of grace and love. In so doing, we will become vessels of God's love, writes Blessed Edith Stein:

> *an overflowing love which wants nothing for itself but bestows itself freely; mercifully, it bends down to everyone who is in need, healing the sick and awakening the dead to life, protecting, cherishing, nourishing, teaching, and forming; it is a love which sorrows with the sorrowful and rejoices with the joyful; it serves each human being to attain the end destined for it by the Father.* **In one word, it is the love of the divine Heart.**[16]

And So the Journey Begins ...

In living out this mission through the gift of authentic femininity we will aid humanity in not falling and do much to heal the world. As we pattern ourselves after the Blessed Virgin Mary, the perfect handmaid of the Lord, we will discover what it means to abandon ourselves to the grace of God through receptivity, trust, and surrender.

The rest of this book will outline for us a spiritual path that leads us in the way of abandonment. A way which fills us with the spiritual POWER we need to live out our special call and gift as women. If we follow it, we will become women imbued with the spirit of the gospel. We will be women filled with grace who point the way to the abundant life in Jesus Christ. We will be women who "aid humanity in not falling." We will be women who bring life by answering our call to spiritual motherhood. And in the process we will discover what holy women throughout the ages have always known:

> *The deepest longing of woman's heart is to give herself lovingly, to belong to another, and to possess this other being completely....*

Only God can welcome a person's total surrender in such a way that one does not lose one's soul in the process but wins it. And only God can bestow Himself upon a person so that He fulfills this being completely and loses nothing of Himself in so doing. That is why total surrender ...[is] the only adequate fulfillment possible for woman's yearning.[17]

Come, let us together find the way to total fulfillment.

Prayer: Strength of the Abundant Life

*A*s I sit now writing this chapter, I gaze upon the awesome beauty of creation. A cloudless blue sky dips into eternity. Crisp foliage paints the landscape in emerald gem tones. Strong, solid pine trees sway slightly, their long needles responding to the sensual caress of the breeze. Capable branches reach skyward and embrace the warmth of the sun, absorbing its radiant energy to begin the life-producing process of photosynthesis. Outside of my window, creation reflects the majesty and splendor of a God who longs for life-giving intimacy with His creatures.

Only through relationship with Him do we come to discover who we really are. As daughters of the Most High, we are called into the very life of His Only Begotten Son, Jesus Christ. His birth, His passion, His death, His resurrection. As such, we are called to a holiness that is an even greater reflection of the majesty of God than is the beauty of nature.

I have learned in my own life, however, that we cannot begin to reflect the Divine Majesty or answer His holy call unless we choose to know Him. We must desire Him as He desires us—freely and completely, without reservation and without condition. God, in His love for us, has given us free will so that our desire for Him might be pure and genuine. He desires that we lift up our hearts to Him, embrace His holy will, and allow His presence to fill our souls. God wants us to open the door of our hearts that He might enter and have communion with us; and there, in our innermost recesses, like the early dew of a spring morning, His gentle love softens the hardened soil of our hearts, infusing them with life-giving grace. His seed of love, so gently planted within us, takes root; and we, in reflection of the Father, yield a fruitful harvest of love.

The Transforming Power of Prayer

I know of no other way to come to know the Father except through the Son. And I know of no other way to come to know the Son except through prayer. Indeed, in the quiet of our hearts, we experience "every spiritual blessing in the heavenly places" (Eph 1:3). As we sit with Him, His voice speaks; His hand touches; His love embraces. The agony of our fallen condition is soothed. The debris of our spirit is dispatched. And our hearts soar to eternity and taste limitless joy. In Ephesians, St. Paul tells us that even before He created the world, God chose us in Him to be holy and blameless in His sight, to be full of love (see Eph 1:4).

In prayer, we sojourn on a holy road to blamelessness and love. Our own miserable condition, frailties, and weaknesses, all become mitigated in the light of His presence. When touched by God's hand, our pain and suffering take on the brilliance of redemptive grace. Our circumstances are fire-tried gold glowing in the crucible of the Most Sacred Heart. And, in the radiant light of the Morning Star, the voice of God speaks. Our hearts stand still. And the Word is made flesh within us. Thus, we cry out with the apostle Paul, "It is no longer I who live, but Christ who lives in me" (Gal 2:20).

Indeed, prayer is the strength of the abundant life. Whether the time is spent quietly adoring the One who made us or storming the gates of heaven with our most urgent petitions or meditatively reading Sacred Scripture, prayer is the transforming agent of our lives. It is so essential to our life in God that both this chapter and the next will be dedicated to it.

The Intimacy of Relationship

I remember so well falling in love with my husband. When we first began to date, I knew there was something special about this person, and about the two of us together. I wanted to spend every moment with him; the time between weekends seemed an eternity.

At first, our moments together were awkward. Though attracted to each other, we had the natural concern of being accepted by the other. But then, as our relationship progressed, we grew more comfortable together. We wanted to know everything about each other, and we spent much time talking about our hopes and dreams, our ideas and attitudes, future plans and aspirations, our view of the world and our place in it.

As that first flicker of interest began to burst into the flame of love, our relationship reached a deeper level of intimacy. No longer did it matter what we talked about or where we went. Just being together was enough. We *knew* each other, *understood* each other, *loved* each other. Trust between us had built, we had surrendered our hearts, and we were receptive to the person of the other. Gradually, evenings yielded to comfortable moments of stillness and silence. The touch of a hand, a gentle smile, the expression in our eyes spoke the intention of our hearts. And when the night was over and we kissed goodnight, the warmth of our love remained like a burning ember within us. With expectant faith, we looked forward to the moment when we would express the fullness of our love as man and wife.

Relationship with God develops much the same way. We cannot begin to know God unless we spend time with Him. The way in which we spend that time is through prayer.

What Is Prayer?

All prayer is simply a response to God's unconditional love for us and His invitation to experience that love. In prayer, God lifts our hearts and minds to Him as we desire to completely surrender to His action in us. Through prayer, God calls us into intimacy with Him, an intimacy that transforms us, an intimacy that imbues us with His presence, an intimacy that is life-giving.

Through prayer, we enter into the very essence of Trinitarian life and come to experience the divine flame of love deep within the inner confines of our being. In union with God through prayer, we become a radiant image of His life active in the world, igniting it with the fire of His presence and healing it with His love.

Starting a Daily Prayer Time

Spiritual maturity comes through prayer and the application of its fruits to our daily lives. A regular time that we set aside each day will help us in our commitment to be earnest and fervent about our spiritual growth.

Spiritual masters throughout the ages have recommended that we select a time of day for prayer that will consistently work into the routine of our daily lives. Many people prefer the morning hours, while many others find that the best time for them to pray is at the end of the day, when the hustle and bustle of daily living is over. Still others find that a quiet time spent in a secluded spot in the middle of the day provides just the right break to refocus their interior dispositions on the things of God. Those who are at home with children may find that their daily prayer time needs to be flexible in light of the day's activities. In any case, we should be faithful to a time of prayer no matter when it occurs in the course of the day.

How Do We Pray?

Each of us has the capacity to pray. Because God wants us to be in relationship with Him, He does not make prayer so difficult and complicated that only the most brilliant and diligent can succeed. In His love and mercy, He grants us all the ability to pray.

There are three main categories of prayer—vocal prayer, meditation, and contemplation. All three are important at every stage of the spiritual life. But, as we progress in the way of prayer, we will experience them at differing levels. Just as a hiker ascends a mountain and sees the landscape he has left behind from a new vantage point, perhaps noticing nuances that eluded him below, or appreciating the scene more fully having achieved a broader perspective, so too will one who is faithful to prayer appreciate an ever-expanding experience of the categories of prayer. Good meditation will produce more fervent vocal prayer; the fruit of contemplation will lead to a richer time of meditation; and fervent oral prayer and rich meditation make good preparation for a more intimate and deeper contemplation.

Let's take a look at each of these categories of prayer and see how we can implement them in our lives.

Vocal Prayer

This first category of prayer can be subdivided into formulated vocal prayer and spontaneous vocal prayer.

Formulated vocal prayer. Formulated prayers use words that have been developed beforehand. Examples include the Hail Mary, the Our Father, the prayers of the Holy Sacrifice of the Mass, the Rosary, and the Liturgy of the Hours. Formulated vocal prayers can be recited alone or with others. These prayers, when offered to God with reverence, devotion, and attention, will stir within us a desire to enter more deeply into the life of God.

A thoughtful, reverent attitude of the heart is of utmost importance when we enter into vocal prayer. Jesus Himself admonished His disciples on the importance of praying with the heart and not just the mouth: "In praying, do not babble like the pagans, who think that they will be heard because of their many words. Do not be like them" (Mt 6:7-8, NAB).

We must evaluate for ourselves whether we are truly praying or simply reciting words. If our desire to grow closer to God is not growing greater, we need to unite ourselves more faithfully to the words we are saying. As we grow in desire for God, our natural yearning will be to spend more time with Him and to come to know Him more intimately. These growing desires for God tell us that our love for Him is deepening and signal that our prayer life is expanding. It is often at this point that we experience the second type of vocal prayer, spontaneous vocal prayer.

Spontaneous vocal prayer. As our love for God grows and develops, we desire to express it to Him in sentiments and emotions which rise up out of our own hearts and minds. These prayers, spoken in our own words, are called spontaneous prayers. Sometimes our spontaneous prayer is expressed in short ejaculations which punctuate our daily activities—*Thank you, Jesus; Have mercy on me, Lord; Dear God, give me patience and grace.* Sometimes it forms the portion of our prayer time when we praise God or thank Him for favors we have received. In group settings like a prayer meeting or a time of praise at a conference, our spontaneous prayer may be joined to that of others.

As we grow more comfortable with spontaneous prayer, we soon desire to spend longer periods of time speaking with God. We want to share with Him our trials and struggles and talk with Him about major decisions to be made. We want to tell Him our true inner thoughts, make Him privy to the deepest parts of our hearts, share with Him those areas within us that are broken and need His healing touch. As we pray in this way, we discover that our time with God produces precious fruit: a deep assurance of His great love for us and a growing awareness of our love for Him.

Gradually, our conversation with God becomes less verbal and more interior. Though we still use words to express our thoughts, we notice that our time of prayer becomes marked by lengthening periods of silence as we quietly wait to hear God's voice speaking to us. This is right because our conversation with Him is to be a dialogue, not a monologue. If we are to hear the voice of God whispering within us, we must quiet ourselves. We must cultivate the gift of listening. And, as our listening skills develop, God's voice can be heard deep within our hearts even in the midst of activity and noise.

This interior exchange between us and God is sometimes called *mental prayer*. St. Teresa of Avila tells us, "Mental prayer is, as I see it, simply a friendly intercourse and frequent solitary conversation with Him who, as we know, loves us."[1] Mental prayer marks a significant deepening of our prayer experience and leads us along the way of prayer.

As with formulated vocal prayer, spontaneous vocal prayer must engage the mind, the heart, and the will. It does no good to "say" prayers or to make pious and sentimental statements. Our prayers must be defined by a desire to conform all aspects of our being to the movement of God's grace within us. Therefore, in prayer we must be present to God in body, mind, and spirit as He moves us forward to the central reality of a life of faith—Christ living in us. It is this to which we are called. And it is only as God's grace accomplishes this in us that we grow to full stature in Christ Jesus.

Meditation on the Word of God

The *Catechism of the Catholic Church* tells us that meditation is a spiritual quest in which the mind desires to understand the Christian life so as to conform and respond to what the Lord is asking (#2705). Christian meditation involves four faculties of the human person—his capacity to think, his imagination, his emotion, and his desire (#2708). All true Christian meditation has the Word of God at its core. Sacred Scripture is God's revelation of Himself, and so it is one of the most important ways He speaks to us. With each reading, God instructs us, guides us, leads us, and answers our deepest needs.

One Christian writer explains the centrality of the Scriptures this way: "Even though they have been fixed in their phrasing for thousands of years, He Who makes us hear them today already had us in mind when He inspired them of old, and He is always present to address Himself to us through them, as if they were at this instant pronounced for the first time."[2]

How, then, can we use Sacred Scripture as a means of entering into prayer?

First, prepare to meet with God. Come to your time of prayer with expectant faith, knowing that this prayerful meditation on the Word of God will yield fruit in your life even if it is not immediately apparent. We lift our hearts and minds to the Lord, humbly offering Him our weaknesses and strengths, our abilities and frailties, our woundedness and fears.

Before beginning, it's important to free ourselves from any distractions. In Matthew 6:6, Jesus tells us, "But when you pray, go to your room and shut the door and pray to your Father who is in secret; and your Father who sees in secret will reward you." We must shut the door on all unnecessary interferences—telephones, televisions, radios, and other interruptions—and free ourselves from interior attitudes that might hinder prayer.

Next, select a Scripture passage upon which to meditate. There is no right or wrong way to choose the passage. Some people prefer to use the liturgical readings of the day. Others may follow a Scripture guide that is recommended through a particular course of study. Still others may choose to read a book of the Bible sequentially, taking a different chapter each day. And finally, some prefer to open the Bible at random and begin to read where their eyes fall.

The passage need not be lengthy, for our goal is not to make progress reading the Bible, but to make progress in our relationship with God. We want to savor every word presented to us in the passage as if it were coming directly from the mouth of God for our ears alone.

Pray to the Holy Spirit to lead and guide you in this time of prayerful reading. Ask Him to remove any interior obstacles or blocks that might prevent you from hearing the Word of God. Ask Him to allow the passage of Scripture to lead you ever more deeply into the Divine Heart. Then, read the passage slowly and carefully, making yourself fully present to the Word in an act of faith. As one spiritual master reminds us:

> *While reading, we should be all adherence, all abandonment, all self-donation, in this faith, to what we hear and to Him Whom we*

hear behind the words being read or reread…. If we believe, as we ought, that the Word is addressed to us, to each of us, in continuing reality here and now, we must also believe that it takes into account everything we are, with all our problems, our needs, our deficiencies, and our joys as well, everything that oppresses or gladdens us, everything we do or fail to do…. The word we read is not made to remain in the head, but to descend into the heart,… that intimate sanctuary in which our eternity is at stake because here is where our ultimate decisions are woven and taken.[3]

We must allow ourselves to be penetrated by the Divine Word, pierced to the core of our being with Divine Love, infused with the very presence of God. We must beg God to reveal in His light what has been hidden in darkness within us. In short, we must permit the Spirit of God to flow in us and through us, rereading our passage as often as necessary so that its full import may be rooted in our heart.

When God's Word is "silent." Most Christians experience "dry" times in their walk with the Lord, times when His message eludes them. If this happens, we can glean from the passage all that God intends by asking ourselves questions as we read.

- "What does this passage mean?"
- "What is happening in it?"
- "What is God saying? To whom is He saying it?"
- "Given my current circumstance or situation, what is God saying to me personally? What grace is He offering me through these words? A promise? A resolution? Hope?"
- Finally, "What sentiments or emotions does this passage draw from me? What causes me to feel as I do? How do I wish to respond to the generosity of God's grace?"

Using these questions as a starting point, we come to be absorbed by the Word of God, and its life begins to generate new life within us.

The Vatican II document on Divine Revelation tells us, "In the sacred books the Father who is in Heaven comes lovingly to meet his children, and talks with them. And such is the force and power of the Word of God that it can serve the Church as her support and vigour, and the children of the Church as strength for their faith, food for the soul, and a pure and lasting fount of spiritual life."[4]

Contemplation—The Divine Life Within

St. Francis de Sales says, "Prayer is called meditation until it has produced the honey of devotion; after that it changes into contemplation."[5] We know that our meditation has produced the "honey of devotion" when our prayer becomes punctuated by impulses of love toward God that grow in intensity and frequency. These loving impulses signal a deepening of our prayer life and are the precursors to a more intimate loving union with God. This loving union finds its fulfillment in contemplation, which is the ultimate goal of the soul's quest for God.

In this form of mental prayer, "the mind is not so much reasoning about God as looking at God in simple faith and adoration.... To contemplate is to see God with the eyes of faith."[6] As in any loving relationship, the more time we spend gazing into the eyes of the beloved, the more deeply in love we become. Father Thomas Dubay refers to this depth of devotion as "a knowing loving that we cannot produce but only receive.... It is a wordless awareness and love that we of ourselves cannot initiate or prolong."[7]

Contemplation differs from meditation in three distinct ways. Meditation is a form of prayer that uses our intellect to stimulate our affections for God. In this sense, meditation is a preparation to the act of loving God. Contemplation, on the other hand, presupposes our love and moves us forward from this point.

Secondly, in meditation we consider the smallest of details as we progress in love of God, much as someone who is falling in love enumerates the attributes that attract her to the other—his goodness, his wisdom, his faithfulness. In contemplation, however, our loving gaze rests on the One we love, no longer lingering over one detail or another. Now, only one thing is important—to be with the One we love.

Finally, while meditation requires much cooperation and effort on our part, in contemplation all depends on God. St. Francis de Sales reminds us, "We do not make this recollection by choice, inasmuch as it is not in our power to have it whenever we wish; it does not depend on our care; but God produces it in us when it pleases Him by His most holy grace."[8]

St. Teresa of Avila contrasts the difference between meditation and contemplation with an illustration from nature itself. She compares meditation to watering a huge garden with a draw-well. The gardener must go to the well and laboriously plumb the water from the well's depths to fill a bucket, which he then hauls to the bed and painstakingly pours out upon the flowers. However, even after all of this work, the gardener knows that it requires rains from the heavens to ensure that the crop will receive the abundance of water it needs.

Contemplative prayer, St. Teresa wrote, is like a spring that ascends in the middle of our soul's garden, spraying life-giving water far and wide over the soil of our heart. Spiritual "flowers" of beauty, grace, holiness, truth, and love grow healthy and well in this garden of the soul when they are nourished by the life-giving spring. In addition, this spring of contemplative prayer produces results far more effortlessly and effectively than the "well-water" of meditative prayer. In meditative prayer, much time had been spent on accepting and receiving God's love, and fashioning appropriate responses to it. In contemplative prayer, God's love inhabits the soul, transforming everything it touches with grace and new life. The soul senses that this love is what it has been called to experience from its inception, and all of its prayer and effort has been leading it to this moment.

While God can and will give such a favor to whomever He chooses, it seems that He most usually gives the favor of contemplation to those who have been faithful to a life of prayerful meditation and virtuous living for some time.

The Transforming Power of Mystical Union

In *Fire Within,* Thomas Dubay, S.M., tells us that the experience of contemplative prayer may vary. He says, "At times this is a delightful, loving attention, at times a dry purifying desire, at other times a strong thirsting for Him. In the beginnings it is usually delicate and brief, but as it develops it becomes burning, powerful, absorbing, prolonged. Always it is transformative of the person."[9]

This quotation tells us that the divine infusions of grace given through contemplative prayer may vary in quality, intensity, and duration. The infusion of contemplation can be delicate or strong, subtle or intense. It may last for a few fleeting seconds or take us to the heights for an hour, a day, a week. Throughout a lifetime, all ranges of variation may be experienced. It is always the Lord who decides what is needed, how it is needed, and to what extent it is needed.

No matter the fluctuations in experience, contemplative prayer tends toward progress, taking us into an ever-deepening experience of prayer. Eventually, it can lead to mystical union—a "secret union" with God that takes place in the very center of our soul.

A number of saints recorded their own powerful experiences of this mystical union with God. Consider these words of St. Thérèse of Lisieux, known as the "Little Flower." She relates her own experience of contemplative prayer and the spiritual marriage in her autobiography, *Story of a Soul:*

> *A few days after my oblation to God's Merciful Love, I had commenced in the Choir the Way of the Cross, when I felt myself suddenly wounded by a dart of fire so ardent that I thought I must die. I know not how to describe this transport; there is no comparison which would make one understand the intensity of that flame. An invisible power seemed to plunge me wholly into fire ... but oh! what fire! what sweetness!*

When her Mother Prioress asked her whether this transport was the first in her life she said:

> *Mother, I have several times had transports of love; once especially during my novitiate when I remained one entire week far indeed from this world; for me, there was as it were, a veil thrown over all things of the earth. But I was not consumed by a real flame, I was able to sustain those delights without expecting that their intensity would cause my earthly fetters to snap asunder, whilst on the day of which I speak, one minute, one second more and my soul must have left its prison.... Alas!—and I found myself on earth, and aridity immediately returned to my heart!*[10]

The Call to Contemplative Prayer

All of us have been called to experience contemplative prayer. Louis Bouyer, in his work *Introduction to Spirituality*, tells us that contemplation *is, in truth, germinally present in the most elementary act of Christian faith. And we might say that this seed develops to the degree to which faith conforms us to itself by obedience.... From a meditation more and more oriented towards the mystery of Christ, more and more absorbed in Him, as the whole of life of him who meditates strives to conform itself to Him in faith, contemplation is born, it might be said in some sense, quite naturally—without ceasing to be, for all that, a pure grace, since it is nothing other than grace making itself felt.*[11]

Thomas Dubay, S.M., tells us that there are some traits common to all of the divine infusions of contemplative prayer. These include

- an experience of God's presence either in a loving attention or a dry longing
- the divine infusion of contemplative prayer coming wholly through God's action in us
- fluctuations in the intensity of our time with God and a diversity in the way in which God makes His presence known and felt
- a deepening of our understanding or knowledge of God and a keener insight into the divine mysteries
- growth in virtue and holiness.[12]

A note of caution is needed here. We should never strive to seek the consolations of God; our quest is for the God of consolation. Should we begin to discover that our thirst is for mystical phenomena, spiritual experiences, or ecstasies, we are sure to slip into a false mysticism that endangers the soul and sets us backward on the road to holiness. All infused contemplation is pure gift. No method, no technique can force the hand of God to give it to us. To think so is prideful and pernicious.

The true mystic desires only to be attached to God, the Source of all life. Franz M. Moschner, in his classic work *Christian Prayer,* writes these words of warning:

> *On the inner journey we must never cast around for discoveries, never in eager curiosity wait for phenomena, sensations, encounters. We would immediately falsify and disrupt our attitude to God and would thus produce in ourselves effects directly opposite to what contemplative prayer is meant to achieve. With categorical firmness we must suppress all and any craving for disclosures, for individual truths, and certainly for personal revelations, otherwise we shall at this point be open to diabolical allurement.*[13]

St. Teresa of Avila tells us that the only desire we should bring to prayer is love. Using the analogy of the rooms in a castle to describe the various stages of mystical prayer, she concludes, "If you would progress a long way on this road and ascend to the Mansions of your desire, the important thing is not to think much, but to love much." [14]

The Effects of Prayer

Encounters with God are life-changing. Because prayer engages us in an intimate relationship with God, prayer is transformative. And its effects are readily seen.

Take, for example, the encounter between Jesus and the demoniac from Gerasene described in the eighth chapter of the Gospel of Luke. Jesus had been traveling by boat to the other side of the Sea of Galilee. When He and the disciples landed on the shore of Gerasene, he was met by a man from the town who was possessed by demons. The naked man approached Jesus, then shrieked, fell to the ground, and cried out, "What have you to do with me,

Jesus, Son of the Most High God? I beseech you, do not torment me." The demons had taken hold of the man many times in the past, which prompted others to restrain the man with chains and fetters. But the man would break his bonds, and the demons would drive him to desolate places. In fact, he had made his home among the tombstones.

As He cast out the demons, Jesus asked them to identify themselves. "Legion," came the response, indicating that the spirits were many. Because they pleaded with Jesus not to drive them back into the abyss, He ordered them into a herd of swine that was feeding nearby instead. The spirits came out of the man and went into the two thousand pigs, which stampeded down the hillside and flung themselves into a nearby lake.

When the swineherds saw what had happened, they ran into the town to spread the news. People from all over the countryside came to see for themselves what had taken place. Coming upon the scene, they hardly recognized the former madman, who sat at the feet of the Lord, fully dressed and in complete command of his senses.

Shortly thereafter, the townspeople asked Jesus to leave. Not only were they terrified by the cure itself, but they were worried that future cures might cost them more than they had already lost in the herd that had drowned. The man from whom the demons had departed, however, understood the great favor he had received from the hand of the Lord. He asked Jesus if he could go with Him, but Jesus sent him away with these words, "Return to your home, and declare how much God has done for you." The man went throughout the town telling everyone how Jesus had delivered him (see Lk 8:26-39).

For the demoniac, this encounter with Jesus was life-changing and transformative. Not only was the man delivered from the demons that had tormented him, but he was also restored to full dignity in the sight of God. No longer was he naked and out of his mind. Now, he was clothed and in command of his senses. Scripture tells us the man sat at the feet of the Lord, a sign of submission and intimacy. Though Scripture does not record the conversation between the two, we know that Jesus' words had a profound effect on the man, so much so that he wanted to be counted among His followers. But, instead, Jesus sent the man back to his hometown to proclaim the healing love of the Lord to all who would listen.

Receive the Healing Touch of Jesus

Each time we encounter Him, the Lord brings healing and wholeness to us, just as He did to the man of Gerasene. The healing love of God permeates our being and sets us free from all that holds us captive, from all that corrupts, from all that robs us of our dignity as children of God. He longs to clothe our spiritual nakedness with the royal robes of grace and love. He desires to lead us out from the "tombstones" of our solitude and desolation and bring us into the light of His presence.

Ridding us of the confusion of sin, the torment of lust, the debris of jealousy, anger, and resentment, He wants to return us to our sensibilities, sensibilities that are the fruit of God's Spirit—love, joy, peace, patient endurance, kindness, generosity, faith, mildness, and chastity (see Gal 5:22). God wants to restore us, to make us whole, to heal us, that we might be the sign of His love in the world. He desires that, like the demoniac, we go into the world proclaiming His healing love to all who will listen. This is the transformation that prayer brings to us. This is the "new man" who is recreated in the radiant splendor of God's love. This is what union with God is all about—knowing God, accepting His love, being transformed by His grace, and sharing His presence with others.

In the next chapter, we will talk about the four movements of prayer and how they release this power of God's life in us, making it active in our lives and the lives of others.

Praise and Petition, Thanksgiving and Contrition: Symphony of the Abundant Life

Our times of prayer and encounters with God are meant to be transforming moments in our lives. Their purpose is to produce within us sanctifying grace and the ability to lead a virtuous life. When we cooperate with the grace we receive in prayer, not only do we become transformed into the image and likeness of God, but our very presence becomes a conduit through which the love of God flows into the world.

If we are to experience the authenticity of our femininity, living out God's call for us to "aid humanity in not falling," we must commit ourselves to a regular time of prayer and develop an attitude of prayer throughout the day. Prayer must become the "song of our heart."

But how can we be in a constant state of prayer and still be busy about the duties of everyday life? St. Paul suggests the answer. He tells us, "Be filled with the Spirit, addressing one another in psalms and hymns and spiritual songs, singing and making melody to the Lord with all your heart, always and for everything giving thanks in the name of our Lord Jesus Christ to God the Father" (Eph 5:18-20).

This passage hints as to how we can make each day of our lives a symphony of prayer, a melody of love, which rises from the depths of our being to the throne of the Father in praise and worship of Him. As is the case with most symphonies, our symphony of prayer is orchestrated around four movements or dispositions of the heart.

The Four "Movements" of Prayer

Many of the great spiritual masters have recommended that we compose our daily lives around four main attitudes of the heart. Some people find it helpful to remember these four interior dispositions with the word "**ACTS**": adoration, contrition, thanksgiving, and supplication.

Adoration

The first movement in our symphony of prayer is adoration. Perhaps we sing praises to God, or simply cry out with the Cherubim and Seraphim, *"Holy, holy, holy is the Lord."* How can we do otherwise than adore the One who bids us enter into sweet communion with Him? We adore God, the Creator, the Supreme Being, the One who gives us life. We tell Him of our love. We do this not because God needs to hear it, but rather because we need to remind ourselves of whose presence we are in. As we lift our minds and hearts to God in adoration of Him, the tempo of our spirits is quickened and invigorated with divine love. New life surges within us and we are made ready to be His instrument in the world.

Contrition

As we worship God, ever more mindful of His holiness and majesty, we become that much more aware of our own faults, and how many of our troubles come from our own sinfulness, weakness, and frailty. True sorrow permeates our being as we implore God to strengthen us against all areas of known temptation as well as those areas of weakness that are still hidden to us. We acknowledge our willful wrongdoing, and try to make reparation for our sins so that they no longer hinder us nor affect others.

This part of our symphony is most important, for only through the plaintive cry of repentance can we come to experience the plenitude of God's mercy and love for us. And only then can we extend His love and mercy to others, refreshing their souls with God's harmony of love.

Thanksgiving

The third movement of our symphony flows from a heart which has been bathed in God's mercy. Bubbling up in us with effervescent joy is gratitude. Real gratitude to God for all that He has done for us. Gratitude for His mercy and kindness. For His love and His peace. Gratitude even for those instances in our lives that at first seem bereft of blessing. Even in these dark times, God's providential hand can be felt, for "we know that all things work for good for those who love God, who are called according to his purpose" (Rom 8:28, NAB). Gratitude of heart produces within us the divine fruit of joy, patient endurance, hope, and trust in God. Our spirits, tuned to a fine pitch with these attributes, become a leitmotif bringing a harmonic cadence to the discordance of the world.

Supplication

Full of expectant faith and confidence in God, we reach the next movement in our symphony of prayer. With true appreciation of how much God loves us, we ask Him to hear our needs as we intercede for ourselves and for others. We petition Him to make haste to help us as we struggle in times of difficulty, travail, and pain; in moments of sadness, grief, and oppression. But our supplication is already imbued with triumph, for "in all these things we are more than conquerors through him who loved us" (Rom 8:37). We are assured of God's help and abiding presence.

St. John Vianney, commonly known as the Curé of Ars, tells us, "God has never refused anything and will refuse nothing to those who ask his grace in the proper way. Prayer is the great means we have for overcoming sin, for persevering in grace, for turning our hearts to God and drawing down upon us all kinds of blessings, whether for our souls or for our temporal needs."[1]

Adoration, contrition, thanksgiving, and supplication—these are the four movements in our symphony of prayer. May the song of our hearts reach to the very ends of the earth.

Praise the Lord, O My Soul

What is praise of the Lord? First and foremost, praise is a form of prayer. Though it may often be expressed with great feeling and fervency, it is rooted in the will—a decision to praise God—rather than in the emotions. We praise God because He deserves it. As we read in the *Catechism of the Catholic Church*, "[Praise] lauds God for his own sake and gives him glory, quite beyond what he does, but simply because HE IS" (#2639).

When we adore God, we are making a statement about who He is and who we are. He is the Creator; we are the created. He is the Life-Giver; we are the ones to whom He has given life. He is the One who Saves; we are the ones in need of salvation.

Why Do We Praise God?

Our praises add nothing to the glory of God, nor does God need our praises. However, praise releases an interior dynamic that lifts us above ourselves and places us in right relationship with our Creator. We praise God not because He needs it, but because *we* need it. Praising God benefits us greatly.

Praise brings us into the presence of God. In Psalm 22:3 we read that God inhabits (or is "enthroned upon") the praises of His people. When we praise God, He makes Himself present to us. He dwells in our praise, and His very life begins to inhabit us. Sincere praise of God opens the door of our hearts so that God can come in and commune with us. Praise is a most effective way to begin a time of prayer.

St. Augustine gives us another reason why we praise God. He tells us, "Our thoughts in this present life should turn on the praise of God, because it is in praising God that we shall rejoice forever in the life to come; and no one can be ready for the next life unless he trains himself for it now."[2]

In praising God now, we are actually training ourselves for the life to come when we will stand before the throne of God crying out, *"Glory to God in the Highest. Holy, holy, holy is the Lord."* Then, our voices will mingle with all the voices in heaven.

But, even in this life, we never praise alone. Because we are part of God's kingdom through our Baptism, our praise already joins the praise of the Heavenly Court, which forever gives glory to God. Rising up like incense before God's throne, our songs of adoration mingle with the alleluias of the angels and the saints, who behold the Beatific Vision.

How, Then, Do We Praise God?

St. Augustine tells us to make certain that our praise comes from our whole being. "See that you praise God not with your lips and voices alone, but with your minds, your lives and all your actions."[3] Praise must be the fundamental attitude upon which we base our lives, and as such, it must permeate all that we think, say, and do.

In this same discourse, St. Augustine tells us that we are not to praise God only when we are assembled together in church, but throughout the rest of our lives as well. We should never cease to praise God. Even when praise does not issue forth from our lips, it should always flow from our hearts, "for as our ears hear each other's voices, so do God's ears hear our thoughts."[4] Scripture offers us many ways in which we can enter into praise (see Col 3:16).

Praising the Lord in song. Singing has always been one of the best ways to praise God. Many times I begin my prayer by singing. I have been known to sing my praises to God as I am driving in the car, cooking in the kitchen, and scrubbing the bathroom. Though my voice is not solo material, God in His mercy receives it anyway and makes this humble offering efficacious in my relationship with Him. Through song I experience the profound presence of God and the healing touch of His love.

As St. Augustine tells us, "He who sings prays twice." Singing in earnest at the Holy Sacrifice of the Mass, singing in unison with brothers and sisters in the Lord at prayer meetings, conferences, and gatherings—in every case the power of the Lord is released when we "lift our hearts to the Lord" in song.

Praying the psalms. Still another way to enter into praise is by uniting ourselves to the prayers of the psalms. The psalms are songs of supplication, thanksgiving, adoration, and praise. Those that particularly express praise to God include Psalms 33–34, 65–66, 95, 100, 103–4, 111, 113, 135, and 148–50. Any one of these could provide fruitful contemplation on the glory of God for many days!

The Liturgy of the Hours, the official prayer of the Church, uses the psalms throughout the day as a means of entering into continual praise of God. If you have not begun to use the rich resource of the psalms in your daily life, I suggest you treat yourself to this wonderful treasure.

Spontaneous expressions of love. Yet another way to praise God is by simply telling Him of our love. Just as we never grow tired of hearing words of affection, so God never tires of it. By expressing to Him how much we love Him, we remind ourselves of our dependency upon Him, of His mercy toward us, and of our desire to bring everything in our lives into conformity with His divine will.

The great saints all spent much time in praise and adoration of God. Consider these prayers of praise and love spoken to God:

Late have I loved you, O Beauty ever ancient, ever new, late have I loved you! You were within me, but I was outside, and it was there that I searched for you.... You called, you shouted, and you broke through my deafness. You flashed, you shone, and you dispelled my blindness. You breathed your fragrance on me; I drew in breath and now I pant for you. I have tasted you, now I hunger and thirst for more. You touched me, and I burned for your peace.[5]

ST. AUGUSTINE

O abyss! O eternal Godhead! O deep sea! What more could you have given me than the gift of your very self? ... In your light you have made me know your truth.... Good above every good, joyous Good, Good beyond measure and understanding! Beauty above all beauty.... You who are the angels' food are given to humans with burning love. You, garment who covers all nakedness, pasture the starving within your sweetness, for you are sweet without trace of bitterness.[6]

ST. CATHERINE OF SIENA

Praise the Lord from the heavens,
    praise him in the heights!
Praise him, all his angels,
    praise him all his host!
Praise him, sun and moon,
    praise him, all you shining stars!
Praise him, you highest heavens,
    and you waters above the heavens!
Let them praise the name of the Lord!   PSALM 148:1-5

The Sacrifice of Praise

Most of us agree that it is easy to praise God when everything is going well in our lives. But what about praising God in difficulty, trial, and tribulation? In these times, praising God is often the last thing we may think about. But it is precisely in these times that praise is most important.

Many years ago I read a book which put forth the premise that we should praise God for all things. The author maintained that by praising God for difficult circumstances and trials, our problems could be transformed. I can remember that as I read this book I thought the idea seemed unreasonable. Did he mean that we were to praise God for illness; marital troubles; financial problems; and difficulties with children, family members, and friends? In fact, this was exactly what he meant. His rationale was that God permits everything to happen to us for our benefit.[7]

As I advanced in my spiritual walk, I began to see that there was wisdom in his words. I discovered that many of the great saints and mystics also advise us to thank God for everything. But what I ultimately came to discover was that our praise of God doesn't transform the situation as much as it transforms *us*.

What is it about praising God in the midst of a trial that is so transforming? First, as we have already mentioned, God inhabits the praises of his people. When God is with us, our hearts, minds, and spirits are elevated. Lifted by the power of His Holy Spirit, we function above the circumstance rather than under it. As the life of God penetrates our being, faith enkindles, trust ignites, and God's own love burns in our soul. Thus, with certitude we cry out, "Who shall separate us from the love of Christ? Shall tribulation, or distress, or persecution, or famine, or nakedness, or peril, or sword?... No, in all these things we are more than conquerors through him who loved us" (Rom 8:35, 37).

Second, as we praise God for the difficulties we face, our attention is no longer focused on ourselves and our problems, but rather on the grace and mercy of God. We begin to see the enormity of His love for us and we ask ourselves how we can love Him more. Through praise, our problem becomes a springboard for deeper union with God. And through deeper union, we become transformed.

St. Augustine tells us, "Our pilgrimage on earth cannot be exempt from trial. We progress by means of trial. No one knows himself except through trial, or receives a crown except after the victory, or strives except against an enemy or temptation."[8] We praise God because our struggle becomes an opportunity for great growth.

We also praise God in the midst of struggle because trials force us to look honestly at ourselves. Our faults and weaknesses stand out in stark relief against the backdrop of pain or inconvenience, tension or stress. Can we offer God a sacrifice of praise by repenting for these faults and sins, for our grudges and temper? Can we praise Him for bringing these frailties to our attention that we might repent? What virtues can we practice to mitigate these faults and weaknesses? We ask, *Can I exercise more courage in this situa-*

tion? How about greater trust? Do I need to practice generosity instead of selfishness? What about compassion rather than criticism? Is God permitting this trial so that I might be changed, touched, or healed in a given area?

Our Lord uses these times of adversity to help us grow in virtue and in spiritual strength. "Consider it all joy, my brothers, when you encounter various trials, for you know that the testing of your faith produces perseverance. And let perseverance be perfect, so that you may be perfect and complete, lacking in nothing," says St. James (Jas 1:2-4, NAB).

Finally, we praise God for our difficulties and trials because they unite us to the sufferings of Jesus. St. Paul tells us that we make up in our own bodies what is lacking in the sufferings of Christ (see Col 1:24). By accepting our tribulations with love, hope, and trust, we imitate our Savior whose own passion and death merited eternal life for us. When the storms of life threaten to overtake us, we need to meditate upon the profound nature of this mystery. In so doing, we come to see our suffering as a gift which unites us to the redemptive act—a gift that God can use for our salvation and the salvation of others. This understanding can make our difficulty not only bearable but joyful as well.

Blessed Mariam Baouardy, a Carmelite stigmatic, wrote, "I weep, O Jesus, for not suffering enough for you.... I desire to suffer, to be immolated, crushed, roasted, until the end of the world, for the triumph of the Church. My God, may You be blessed!"[9]

Perhaps we have not yet attained to the self-giving level of Blessed Mariam, but each of us can begin to offer to God all of the inconveniences, disappointments, contradictions, trials, and difficulties that mark our lives, that He might use them for our benefit and the benefit of others.

Thanksgiving: The Song of a Grateful Heart

As we consider the many times we have seen the magnificent glory of God so clearly demonstrated in our lives, our hearts are filled with thanksgiving and gratitude. No practical problem or spiritual difficulty can separate us from God's love (see Rom 8:38-39).

Unlike human love, which can disappoint us, God's love is steady and sure, infinite and everlasting. It is faithful and trustworthy. It is unconditional and free. All God asks us to do is receive it and allow it to transform us.

Once we permit ourselves to revel in this truth, the circumstances of our lives no longer have power over us. Our spiritual vision is restored, the hand of God is revealed, and we come to experience that freedom of spirit, that charism of joy which characterizes the Christ-centered heart. We come to see that God, who is Goodness, radiates goodness to each of us.

Having cultivated a spirit of true gratitude, even in the midst of our greatest trials our hearts are at peace because they rest in the loving embrace of the Sacred Heart. The words *Thanks be to God* fall from our lips with great fervency, for in the words of St. Augustine, "What better words may we carry in our heart, pronounce with our mouth, write with a pen? ... There is no phrase that may be said so readily, that can be heard with greater joy, felt with more emotion or produced with greater effect."[10] What are some of the effects of cultivating a spirit of gratitude? Let's take a look.

Purity of Heart

Gratitude focuses our hearts on God rather than self. Through heartfelt thanksgiving, the soul is freed from introspection, from self-centeredness, from conceit. Gratitude begets generosity of heart, which in turn becomes the catalyst for action in the dealings of daily life. Thus, as selfish motivation yields to godly concern for others, gratitude leads to purity of heart.

Increased Sensitivity to the Action of the Holy Spirit

When it is no longer consumed by selfish wants and desires, the grateful soul distinguishes the many blessings God provides for it each day. The most common experiences of daily life become cause for exultation, while even the darkest moments gleam with the precious gem of joy, afire with the radiant splendor of divine love.

Gradually, the soul becomes docile to the action of the Holy Spirit within it, who fans the flames of expectant faith in a way that makes us ever more sensitive to the consolations of God. "Whoever faithfully cultivates this form of prayer ... will be gladdened by spiritual experiences hitherto unknown."[11]

True Gratitude Leads to Humility

Writing in *Introduction to the Devout Life*, St. Francis de Sales tells us, "the lively consideration of graces received makes us humble because a knowledge of them excites gratitude."[12]

As we see the hand of God in daily life and feel His tender consolation within the inner recesses of our soul, we become increasingly aware of our own sinfulness. The frailty and unworthiness of our human nature stand out in stark relief against the perfection of the One who is Ultimate Love, Infinite Goodness, Eternal Majesty. We see the chasm that separates the created from the Creator, and our hearts would languish if at the same time we did not see the Act that bridges the gap, God's ultimate act of love: the Passion, death, and resurrection of His Son, our Lord Jesus Christ.

It is indeed the love of God that saves us. It is indeed the grace of God that redeems us. It is indeed the Person of God who is our Salvation. All that we are, all that we have, comes to us from God.

In ourselves we are nothing, but through God every spiritual blessing in the heavens is ours.

How deeply, how richly we are loved by God! He is the sustenance of our life. He is the Soul of our soul.

How, Then, Do We Cultivate Gratitude?

One day I received a letter at the ministry. It was from a woman who was responding to a small card I had included in the monthly letter I send out to those who support the efforts of *Living His Life Abundantly*. This little card popped open to reveal a Scripture passage. In my letter, I had suggested that the Holy Spirit would give a special word to each individual through the passage he or she received. This is what the woman wrote to me:

Dear Johnnette,

I truly enjoyed your newsletter and the little pop-open card with a scripture passage. I am a sixty-eight-year-old widow, mother of six children and I have eighteen grandchildren. I know I am very blessed by God with a beautiful family. I grew up in a family of ten children, and after raising six children of my own, with hustle and bustle all my life, now I live alone and at times it is very lonely. I have to pray hard and really work at it so as not to become depressed.

On Saturday, your newsletter came to my home. That same day I had a telephone call from a shut-in member of our parish, asking me if I would pick her up and take her to Saturday evening Mass. I said "Yes" I would take her. My parish ministry is taking Holy Communion to shut-in members and visiting them.

When I came home from evening Mass the thought went through my mind, with somewhat of a heavy heart, "Thank God I was needed tonight. My family doesn't need me anymore." At that very time I noticed my mail lying on the kitchen table and I opened your newsletter. The first thing I read was the scripture passage. On the left-hand side of the card it said, "I am needed," and the scripture passage read, "For I know well the plans I have for you—plans to give you hope and a future"—Jeremiah 29:11.

This passage for sure was hand-picked for me by the Holy Spirit. I felt an uplifting, that God really loves me and is looking out for me. This surely was a moment of grace for me. I was actually stunned for a moment. I have prayed this passage over and over since that day and meditate on it.

Gratefully,

This woman's letter outlines the way to grow in the virtue of gratitude.

First, she counted her blessings. She saw God's blessings in her children and her grandchildren. "There is no one who, with a little bit of thought, cannot but discover many reasons for being grateful to God…. Once we have come to an appreciation of all He has given to us, we will have abundant cause to give thanks continually."[13] God has blessed each of us in many ways. Counting our blessings is a sure way to experience real gratitude.

Second, she became involved in service to others. Whether we take Holy Communion to shut-ins, volunteer as catechists, or serve food to the homeless, participating in the lives of others through charity expands our hearts, helps us to see God in our neighbor, and makes us more grateful for His presence in our lives.

Third, the woman looked for God's intervention in her daily life. She recognized the Scripture passage on the pop-open card as God's own voice speaking to her. Rather than dismissing it as coincidence, she meditated on this word, taking it seriously, letting it build hope and faith within her. In effect, she cooperated with the grace God gave her—even when the going got tough. Taking time to meditate on how God is revealing His presence to us in the midst of struggle gives us the courage and perseverance to go on.

Fourth, her days became characterized by prayer. It is in prayer and through prayer that we come to know the Person of God and the ways of God. It is also in prayer that we are healed, restored, and made whole spiritually and emotionally. Our awareness of God increases when we utter short spontaneous prayers in the midst of daily activity. These ejaculations lift our minds and hearts to God, helping to keep us in an attitude of prayer throughout our day. And, in many cases, they give us the strength to persevere. The woman tells us, "I have to pray hard and really work at it so as not to become depressed." As we have discussed before, prayer helps us cope with our difficult circumstances.

Finally, the woman shared her gratitude to God with me. God's actions in our lives are not meant for us alone. They are meant to be shared with others so that they, too, might come to know His healing love. Recall the Samaritan woman at the well, who, filled with gratitude after meeting Jesus, ran into the town proclaiming the love and generosity of God (see Jn 4:1-30). We can only imagine the number of people who came to Him through her witness.

Our gratitude to God is meant to be a means of bringing others to Him. And yet, as we cultivate a spirit of gratitude—counting our blessings, serving others, looking for God's hand in daily life, spontaneously expressing our thanksgiving to God, and sharing our gratitude with others—we will reap the benefits as well. The daily practice of gratitude makes us sensitive to the guiding hand of the Holy Spirit—in good times and bad.

Petition: The Cry of Our Hearts

She was distraught. Her furrowed brow was etched with worry and concern and her eyes spilled over with tears of fear and pain. She had heard that He was a great healer, a miracle-man, the promised Messiah of the Israelites. She didn't know what reaction He would have toward her, a Canaanite woman, but she knew that she would suffer anything for the sake of her daughter. He had recently been seen in the area of Tyre and Sidon, and she knew she must at least ask Him to help her child. With expectant faith she made her way through the streets, looking for Him.

At last she saw Jesus and His disciples. Presenting herself to Him, she cried out, "Have mercy on me, O Lord, Son of David; my daughter is severely possessed by a demon."

Jesus looked at her, but did not respond. The disciples became troubled by the woman's cries and pleas. "Send her away," they entreated Jesus. "She is shouting after us."

Jesus told the woman that His mission was only to "the lost sheep of the house of Israel," not to Gentiles such as herself. But the woman was undaunted. She knew Jesus could cure her daughter, and she was determined to receive His help.

"Help me, Lord!" she cried.

Jesus responded even more firmly this time, "It is not fair to take the children's bread and throw it to the dogs."

Again, the woman persisted. "Yes, Lord," she begged, "yet even the dogs eat the crumbs that fall from their master's table."

Her faith and perseverance won Jesus' heart. With great tenderness He replied, "O woman, great is your faith! Be it done for you as you desire" (see Mt 15:21-28). In that very moment, her daughter was healed.

We can learn much from the Canaanite woman about prayerful supplication.

- *She recognized Jesus and the source of His power.* By calling Jesus "Lord" and "Son of David," she admitted His identity as the Messiah, even though she herself was not an Israelite. Thus, she invested faith in Him.

  We, too, must recognize the One before whom we place our petitions. We must trust in His omnipotent power and know that He is fully able to respond to all of our needs. Like the Canaanite woman, our disposition of heart must reflect confidence and expectant faith.

- *With clarity, simplicity, and confidence, she presented her need.* The woman did not go into a long description of her daughter's affliction. Nor did she offer the Lord explanations of why she "deserved" this healing. Rather, with straightforward confidence she simply stated her need.

  On some level she must have known that God wants only good things for His children, even those who are not officially part of the "flock." She was right.

  In the Gospel of Matthew, Jesus emphasizes God's desire to give His children good things. "Which one of you would hand his son a stone when he asks for a loaf of bread, or a snake when he asks for a fish? If you then, who are wicked, know how to give good gifts to your children, how much more will your heavenly Father give good things to those who ask him" (Mt 7:9-11, NAB).

  When we express our need to God with childlike trust, we are acknowledging that He is a loving Father who desires only good things for us. With the same childlike trust, we must have confidence that His answer to our prayer will come in precisely the way that is best for us.

- *The woman humbly persevered even in the face of obstacles.* When the woman did not immediately receive the answer she had hoped for, she did not give up or run away dejected, sad, or angry. Instead, she persisted in asking the Lord to grant her favor. She continued to earnestly beseech Him even when He seemed silent, unresponsive, and discouraging. She trusted that He knew her heart and would meet her need. And, ultimately, He did.

We, too, must have a persevering attitude in prayer. When our prayers are not answered as quickly as we would like or in the way we would like, we must remember that God's ways are perfect. We see so little with our finite minds, but God sees the eternal consequences of everything. We must trust in His omniscience.

Misconceptions and Misunderstandings About Praying for Our Own Needs

Most of us have no trouble asking God for His help on behalf of another. However, many Christians find it hard to come to God with their own needs. In this section we'll take a look at some of the common misconceptions people have about this important aspect of prayer.

Feelings of unworthiness can rob us of our boldness in prayer. So many times I have heard people remark that they only petition God for the needs of others rather than their own needs. Perhaps they don't think their needs are worthy of God's attention. Perhaps they think they can handle things on their own, saving their petition "quota" for the truly dire emergencies. These attitudes of heart do not come from God. They are most likely rooted in pride, presumption, or a poor understanding of God's love for us. While interceding for others is part of our Christian obligation, *we err by not asking the Father to meet our needs as well.*

Jesus tells us in St. Matthew's Gospel, "Ask, and it will be given you; seek, and you will find; knock, and it will be opened to you. For everyone who asks receives, and he who seeks finds, and to him who knocks it will be opened" (Mt 7:7-8). It is difficult to get much plainer than that. God *wants* us to ask Him to meet our needs and He wants to heal us of anything that would prevent us from doing so.

Does prayer really change anything? Some individuals assert that since God already knows what is going to happen, prayer won't change anything anyway. The example of the Canaanite woman shows that God is sensitive to our requests, even when the likelihood of a positive response seems slim. The woman was a pagan, one who did not have any reason to expect that the God of the Israelites would hear her prayer and answer it. Yet, because of her faith, perseverance, and humility, God responded to her request.

Speaking to this very question, St. Thomas Aquinas teaches that because God foresees all things, He also foresees our prayers and petitions and incorporates them into the movements of His Spirit in our daily lives as a cause or a motive for His action. From this perspective, our prayers do not change or modify the divine will as much as they merit graces that have already been preordained for us, should we ask for them.[14] St. Paul encourages the Philippians, "Have no anxiety about anything, but in everything by prayer and supplication with thanksgiving let your requests be made known to God" (Phil 4:6).

If God knows all things, then why should we have to pray for our needs—why doesn't He just answer them? God wants us to pray for our needs so that we can see the answer to our prayers as a sign of His love for us. An incident from my own life dramatically illustrates this point.

When our youngest daughter was three years old, she was

bitten in the eye by a dog we had brought home from the animal rescue only a day or so before. Because I did not realize he had been living on the streets, rummaging through garbage cans for his food, I threw away some pork chop bones in the trash can in our kitchen. Smelling the meat, the dog went over to the can. Our little girl walked over to the dog and put her arm around his body in a loving gesture. But the dog, instinctively protecting the food he had found, turned and lunged at the closest thing nearby. In this case, it was our daughter's left eye.

We called 911, applied ice to her eye, and prayed to God that she would be OK. I also called a close friend who was a member of our prayer group, cried out what had happened, and asked her to call others to pray for us.

When we arrived at the hospital, the doctor told us that although our daughter's eye was intact, her eyelid had been all but destroyed. He said she needed surgery, but sadly warned us that the results would not be good. He could use skin from behind her ear to make up for the missing eyelid tissue, but the muscles were so destroyed that she would not have control over the eyelid and it would permanently droop. In addition, because all of the roots of her eyelashes were exposed, she would lose them and they would not grow back.

Though this news was devastating, my husband, daughter, and I experienced great peace; I knew God was at work. Our baby even said that she forgave the dog.

The grueling microsurgery lasted for four hours. Over 150 stitches were sewn into our little girl's eyelid, making it look more like a jigsaw puzzle than a part of her sweet little face. When the doctor came out, the only good news he could offer us was that he didn't have to graft the tissue because he was able to "weave" the stitches together.

However, by the next morning a miracle had begun to happen.

The eyelid was healing so rapidly that the doctor was able to remove some of the stitches immediately. Within a few short days, he had taken out most of them. All that remained were three little stitches along the lash line. This was the site where the tissue was missing and the doctor had woven the stitches together to fill the gap. A small ball of mucus had formed around these stitches to protect the cornea. Because of the location of these sutures, the doctor said they would need to be removed under anesthesia.

One night, as I was giving our daughter her bath, I noticed that the little mucus ball was gone. Tipping her head back to get a better look, I saw that the three stitches had disappeared! I was exuberant by the time my husband came home that evening. Though he appreciated my enthusiasm, he assured me this wasn't possible. The next morning, however, when our baby woke up, he discovered for himself that what I had said was absolutely true. The stitches were gone. What is more, the eyelid was not drooping and our daughter was able to blink it, open it and close it at will.

You can well imagine the surprise and amazement of the doctor when we took our daughter to his office for her appointment. Shocked at what he saw, he at first accused us of taking the stitches out, and then he accused us of taking her to another doctor. We assured him that we had done neither, and that we believed it was a miracle given to us by God. He confirmed that she would have total use of her eyelid and then said, "And by the way, she only seems to have lost one eyelash. I don't think she'll lose any more." And she didn't. Had we not prayed for God's mercy in this situation, we may not have recognized the hand of God in our time of need. Thus, we would have missed one of His greatest blessings for us.

God wants to demonstrate His love for us by responding to the needs we present to him. And, as we see His love respond in one situation, we have the faith and confidence to ask again. "With all prayer and supplication, pray at every opportunity in the Spirit. To that end, be watchful with all perseverance and supplication for all the holy ones," St. Paul tells the Ephesians (6:18, NAB).

Why Does God Sometimes Seem to Delay in Answering Our Prayers?

In our daughter's story, our prayers were answered quickly. This is not always the case. Sometimes we petition God for a long time before a prayer is answered. God does not want us to lose heart. There are several reasons why God does not always answer our prayers immediately.

Sometimes what we are asking of Him is not in our best interests, or in the best interests of the one for whom we are praying. Because we do not have the mind of God, we do not always know the best way to pray for a given situation or circumstance. Therefore, our prayer must always conform to God's holy will. In the Our Father we pray, "Thy will be done." We must trust that God knows best and will meet our every need even if the answer does not come in the way we hope for.

Second, *God sometimes delays in answering so that He can build up our level of faith.* In the story of the Canaanite woman, Jesus' comments to her seem harsh and difficult to accept. Yet, look at what happens to the woman's faith as she persistently continues to ask the Lord for His help. It increases—so much so that she merits exceptional praise from Jesus: "Woman, you have great faith," He tells her.

God desires that we be persistent. Recall the parable that Jesus tells about the necessity of praying always and never losing heart.

"In a certain city there was a judge who neither feared God nor had respect for people. In that city there was a widow who kept coming to him and saying, 'Grant me justice against my opponent.' For a while he refused; but later he said to himself, 'Though I have no fear of God and no respect for anyone, yet because this widow keeps bothering me, I will grant her justice, so that she may not wear me out by continually coming.'" And the Lord said, "Listen to what the unjust judge says. And will God not grant justice to his chosen ones who cry to him day and night? Will he delay long in helping them? I tell you, he will quickly grant justice to them. And yet, when the Son of Man comes, will he find faith on earth?"

LUKE 18:2-8, NRSV

Perhaps our fervent prayer of petition will reassure our Lord that when He does come again, He will at least find faith in us.

Finally, *God will never trespass upon our free will.* It is important to remember this when it comes to understanding God's response to our prayers. When our prayers of petition for someone seem to be going unheard, perhaps it is because in his stubbornness or obstinacy, the person we are praying for is refusing God's grace and love. In these cases it is most important for us to be vigilant and diligent in our prayer of petition.

St. Monica prayed for many years that her son, Augustine, would be converted. She often prayed that God would send others to her son to help him find his way. Because of her persistent prayer, she lived to see her son enter the Faith and use his great intellect to advance the teachings of the Church. We should pray like this, too, especially when we are praying for someone's conversion of heart. "Persevere in prayer. Persevere, even when your efforts seem sterile. Prayer is always fruitful."[15]

Reparation: The Right Attitude to Bring to Prayer

In Psalm 51, the psalmist rightly declares, "A broken and contrite heart, O God, thou wilt not despise."

The *Catechism of the Catholic Church* tells us that true sorrow for our sins is a prerequisite for pure prayer. "A trusting humility brings us back into the light of communion between the Father and His Son Jesus Christ" (#2631).

Here it is helpful to consider what St. Ignatius of Loyola says about two "standards." In his *Spiritual Exercises,* he presents these standards as ways of evaluating the world and ourselves in it.

The first standard is **the way of sin.** It is corrupted by the Fall and the lusts of man. This standard is governed by the Prince of Darkness. Following this standard merits death.

The second standard is **the way of Christ the King.** This standard is characterized by the grace and love of God. To follow it, we strive to bring everything within us under the Lordship of Jesus Christ by following the Commandments, living the Beatitudes, and practicing virtue. The reward for this standard is eternal life.

As children of God, we are called to the standard of Christ the King. We must strive to bring all of our thoughts, words, and deeds into conformity to His will. We must endeavor to root out, by God's grace, anything that is sinful and disordered in our lives. Because we have fallen short of the glory of God, all of us need to experience God's mercy and healing as we approach our time of prayer.

In seeing our own sinful nature and asking forgiveness for our sins, we make progress in the virtue of humility. Through repentance we are reshaped and refashioned according to the standard of Christ so that we might be a *light to the nations.*

But before we can repent, we must answer the question Jesus posed to Peter: *"Who do you say I am?"* He asks.

"Who Do You Say That I Am?"

I remember well my own moment of answering this question. In the summer of 1981 I decided I wanted a career change and made plans to begin insurance school. At the same time I was planning to attend insurance class, a woman whom I knew casually had also registered for the same course. We decided to carpool together.

I discovered that she was going through a difficult divorce, one she did not want. My friend was distraught about her marriage. It was a painful story, and as we would drive the twenty-mile distance to class, she would share her sorrow with me. My heart ached for her, and many of those mornings we both cried as we crossed the sparkling water of Tampa Bay.

It was clear that my friend was in tremendous emotional pain and that her future was uncertain. And yet, by the time we would reach our destination, with eyes smiling through her tears, she would say to me, "But, you know, Johnnette, everything is going to be OK. I know Jesus is in the midst of this." She was certain that God was going to work this whole miserable situation for the good. I soon found myself intrigued by her level of faith.

I had been born and raised a Catholic and had twelve years of parochial education. In my youth, I'd had a tremendous faith in God. I can remember getting up early the first Saturday of each month and walking to our parish church, about a mile and a half away, to make the First Saturday Devotion to the Sacred Hearts of Jesus and Mary.

I had been taught by the Vincentian Sisters of Charity and the Dominicans and, as a child, I could see myself dressed in one of those habits. St. Thérèse, the Little Flower, was my favorite saint, with St. Maria Goretti a close second. I can remember wondering if I would have the courage to give my life for Jesus. I prayed that I would.

But when I graduated from high school in 1968 and went off to Pennsylvania State University, my dreams and aspirations changed dramatically. Vietnam protests flavored the college scene, and campus life was in tumult. Sit-ins, be-ins, and love-ins were the order of the day; parties were the order of the night.

My parents were mortified that the daughter they sent away to college with a lovely wardrobe came home in clothes purchased from the Army-Navy Surplus Store. Contact lenses gave way to wire-rims, a page-boy gave way to a shag, and my Catholic faith gave way to relativism. Initially I experienced a sense of guilt and shame, but I could always quell those feelings with another sit-in, party, or protest.

I was engaged at the time. However, my fiancé enlisted in the army after he received his draft notice, and this put a strain on our relationship. Our worldviews were radically different and seemed irreconcilable. Eventually, we broke our engagement.

It wasn't until the summer before my senior year that I began to get my life back in order. I was haunted by a strange feeling of emptiness. One day I found myself in a State College hangout in the middle of the day. I felt depressed and sad. The darkness of the room gave me a sense of privacy, and I found myself doing something I hadn't done in a long time. I prayed.

Dear God, I began. *I am so confused. I once was so sure of You, and now I don't even know if You exist. Please give me a sign. If You exist and if You love me, let me know. I need You.*

That done, I got up and went outside. It was a glorious spring day. I breathed the flower-scented air deeply, taking in the aromatic fragrance as I walked along the avenue in the brilliant sunshine. *Perhaps everything will work out,* I thought. I threw my head back to let the warmth of the sun dry my tear-stained cheeks, and then I noticed it.

There, in the sky, on this radiant spring afternoon, was a

magnificent rainbow. It hadn't rained. What caused it to appear? And then I remembered my prayer. God had heard me! He did exist and He was showing me His love!

Though I was incredibly moved by this experience, it didn't send me back into the arms of Mother Church. But it did have a profound effect. I changed my daily activities, donned more acceptable garments, and began going home on a regular basis. My parents were thrilled.

I heard that my old boyfriend was being discharged from the army, his enlistment period over, and I thought perhaps I should give him a call. We met for lunch and realized that there was still a flicker of interest between us. We fanned that flicker into a flame: Anthony and I were married two years later.

Though we had been married in the Catholic Church, neither Anthony nor I was practicing our faith. Anthony lost his faith at a Catholic men's college in the wake of Vatican II. My own faith experience hadn't revived from its exposure to the college scene. It wasn't until I gave birth to our first child that we began to think seriously about religion. Though we were not sure if this "religion-thing" was necessary, we decided that our own doubts should not affect the welfare of this precious child—just in case. We had her baptized at the local Catholic church.

Now it was 1981. Three baptized children later, and we were still for the most part nonpracticing Catholics. I had begun to go back to Sunday Mass during Lent of that year. I didn't know why, but I just felt that I should. Though my husband didn't join me, I did take our six-year-old along. It was getting difficult to answer all of her questions each Sunday, especially since I didn't know what I believed anymore, but I continued to go to Mass and my daughter continued to go with me.

That was the status of my faith as I headed to insurance school each day with my friend. Was I intrigued by her story? You bet. I was fascinated that this woman really thought God could work something good out of her horrible situation. *Where does a person get faith like that?* I wondered. And one day, I wondered the question out loud. It was just the opportunity my friend was waiting for.

She began to share with me about Jesus. She sounded like she knew Him personally. The more she shared with me, the more I experienced a longing to know Him in the same way. The sparkle in her eyes and the excitement in her voice communicated to me that He was well worth knowing.

Our trips to and from Tampa took on a new dimension; I found myself looking forward to them. Then one conversation became a turning point in my life. I told my friend that our talks had given me much food for thought. "I would like to know Jesus like you do," I said to her.

"You would?" she replied.

"Yes, I would."

"Then I have a book for you to read. I'll bring it for you tomorrow," she said with characteristic enthusiasm.

The next morning my friend gave me the slim little volume she had promised. It had been written by a registered nurse who noticed that when she prayed with her patients they were healed. When I asked my friend what that meant, she told me that Jesus heals people today just like He healed people two thousand years ago. I thought that was phenomenal.

But there was more. My friend related that healing was only one gift of the Holy Spirit; there were others, she said, all free for the asking. She sounded pretty convinced about all of this. As for me, I couldn't wait for an opportunity to read this book.

The opportunity came that weekend. The author described many of the experiences she'd had of people being healed through prayer. As I read account after account, my amazement grew. She also spoke about the Holy Spirit in a real and tangible way—as if we could be filled with His power. She used words and phrases like *"inner healing," "gifts of the Holy Spirit," "intercessory prayer."*

I eagerly turned one page after another, my hungry heart feasting on all that I read. The book closed with an invitation to receive the Holy Spirit and enter into a relationship with Jesus Christ. I thought about it for a moment. And then I plunged in. *Lord,* I prayed, *it says in this book that I can enter into relationship with You and be filled with the Holy Spirit.* As I continued to pray, I sensed a deep longing within me. *Lord, I didn't even know how much I wanted to be in relationship with You—not until this minute. I'd like all of the gifts this book mentions, and true faith and forgiveness. Thank You in advance for hearing this prayer, and now I'm going to read the one in the book.*

Tears running down my cheeks, I prayed the prayer of repentance. I thought about all the time I had wasted, all the years that could have been empowered by the presence of God. I thought about many of the decisions I had made—decisions that I regretted. My heart ached that I had chosen against the Lord so many times. And yet, I was aware of the profound mercy of God. How much He must love me to give me this opportunity! How much He must care. He was the one I had been searching for. And that afternoon, I surrendered my heart and soul to Jesus Christ.

Prodigal Daughter, Prodigal Son

My experience is not unique. Our Lord himself told a group of sinners and tax collectors a story about a willful son (see Lk 15:11-32).

In this story, a young man asked his father for his inheritance so that he could leave the restrictions of his father's home and find his own fortune and fame. Within a short time, the young man had squandered all of his money. Furthermore, he was starving. Utterly broke, he found the only work available—taking care of a rich man's swine. Even the pigs' fodder looked like a feast to him.

One day, the young man evaluated his situation. For the first time, he saw himself as his father would see him—a miserable failure, dejected and an object of mockery. He decided to break away, return to his home, and ask his father to forgive him. Though he wasn't sure if his father would receive him with anger or mercy, he knew it could be no worse than his current situation. "At least," he reasoned, "my father's servants have plenty to eat." And so, he trudged dejectedly homeward.

> *While he was still far off, his father saw him and was filled with compassion; he ran and put his arms around him and kissed him. Then the son said to him, "Father, I have sinned against heaven and before you; I am no longer worthy to be called your son." But the father said to his slaves, "Quickly, bring out a robe—the best one—and put it on him; put a ring on his finger and sandals on his feet. And get the fatted calf and kill it, and let us eat and celebrate; for this son of mine was dead and is alive again; he was lost and is found!" And they began to celebrate.*
>
> LUKE 15:20-24, NRSV

The Prodigal Tale Retold

Each one of us is like the Prodigal Son. We have been given a great inheritance by our Father. First, we bear the gift of life and personhood. Made in His image and likeness, we uniquely and individually bear His majesty and splendor. In a most sublime way, as women, He has given us the precious gift of participating in His divine act of creation.

But most of all, God has given to each one of us the gift of salvation. Through the Passion, death, and resurrection of God's only begotten Son, Jesus Christ, the grace of redemption has been poured upon all who are baptized. And yet, in so many ways, we have squandered this gift of redemption in willfulness, in stubbornness, in pride and rebellion. We have squandered it on gossip, anger, envy, and greed. We have squandered it on bitterness and resentment, hostility and revenge.

We have squandered it on an array of self-appointed "rights." The "right" to sacrifice virginity for the fleeting satisfaction of a sexual thrill. The "right" to govern our bodies through contraception and sterilization. The "right" to abort our children to rid ourselves of unwanted motherhood.

All of us, in so many ways, have marred the image of God within us. All of us, in so many ways, have threatened our salvation through sin. All of us, in so many ways, have squandered the priceless gift of redemption.

The Prodigal Returns

Perhaps, like the Prodigal Son, we have taken stock of our situation. Perhaps we have seen the misery and pain created by our sinfulness. Perhaps we have seen the devastating effects of our sin on others. And, perhaps, like the Prodigal Son, we wonder if our God will receive us back. We wonder if we will incur wrath or mercy.

But, like the Prodigal Son's father, God our Father waits for our return. He longs for us as a lover pines for his beloved. He tells us in Scripture that He draws us to Himself with bands of love (see Hos 11:4) and that He has never forgotten us (see Is 49:16). And, just as the Prodigal Son's father greets him with mercy and elation, so does our Father in heaven extend infinite mercy and understanding to us, His prodigal children.

There is no sin that is greater than the mercy of God! None. He embraces us with redemptive grace, robes us in infinite mercy, and places a ring of eternal love around our hearts. Our Father in heaven rejoices because His lost child has come home!

How do we respond to such mercy and love? We respond by answering the question of His Son, Jesus Christ, *Who do you say that I am?*

Somehow, we sense that our own identity is intimately connected to the One who poses this question. And, almost instinctively, we know that without Him the emptiness of our hearts will remain, like postpartum clings to the womb. We must say "yes" to this Divine Lover. We must say "yes" to the One who calls us "His beloved."

And so, our response to Jesus' question begins to quake within us. First, as an almost imperceptible tremble, then growing with greater and greater intensity, until the depths of our being explode in reply, *You are the Messiah! You are the Son of God.* And, as these words resonate within us, we are reborn, made new, sanctified.

There can be no growth in holiness until we accept the One who personifies the unconditional love of the Father—Jesus Christ. Through a conscious turning toward God through Jesus Christ, we turn our backs on our sinful ways, on attitudes that do not conform to His holy will, and to our own selfish wants and desires. *Metanoia*, conversion of heart, becomes the rudder of our lives. The *Catechism of the Catholic Church* tells us that "Christ's call to conversion continues to resound in the lives of Christians.... This endeavor of conversion is not just a human work. It is the movement of a 'contrite heart,' drawn and moved by grace to respond to the merciful love of God who loved us first" (#1428).

True conversion of heart means that we submit all our thoughts, words, and actions to the guidance of the Holy Spirit. In so doing, we call ourselves to an accountability that leads to perfection. Unless we can submit ourselves to the discipline of holy perfection, we will never find our true identity as women, we will never reach our fullest potential as individuals, we will never experience intimate union with God.

God our Father tells us, "Sanctify yourselves, then, and be holy; for I, the Lord, your God, am holy" (Lv 20:7, NAB). Each of us is called to follow in the footsteps of Jesus Christ. Each of us is called to sainthood.

As we come to the close of this chapter, it is good for us to reflect upon this question that Jesus poses. Who *do* we say that He is? Is He the Lord of our lives? Have we received Him? Do we trust in Him? Can we surrender to Him? If our answers to these questions come up short, perhaps we should take this opportunity to invite Jesus into the inner recesses of our heart. Thus will we come to know how deeply God loves us, how specifically He has chosen us, and how dramatically He desires to use us as an instrument of love in the world.

Dear Jesus, in my journey through life I have
pridefully followed paths that have led me away from You.

I repent of my sins and I long to come home to You.
Inspired by Your Holy Spirit, I confess that You are the
only begotten Son of God.

I ask You to be the Lord of my life.
Forgive me my sins as I surrender myself to Your healing love.

You are the Way, the Truth, and the Life.
Strengthen me as I seek to place my feet in Your footsteps.

Thank You for Your grace which has brought me
home to You today. Amen.

FOUR

Obedience: Power for the Abundant Life

"Holiness," Pope John Paul II tells us, "...must be the fundamental presupposition, and an irreplaceable condition for everyone in fulfilling the mission of salvation within the Church."[1]

To many of us, the very idea of holiness seems like a goal too lofty to attain. And indeed it is—for us. But with God, all things are possible. The saints in heaven testify that not only can we grow in grace, but we can even attain spiritual perfection through God's action in our soul.

Holiness comes through an intimate relationship with God in which we are transformed by His presence active within us. It is only as we enter the crucible of divine love and allow its penetrating fire to cauterize the inner confines of our heart that we begin to experience His saving power.

Working deep within, God's healing presence dresses the wounds of our fallen condition, binds them up with cords of love, and regenerates them through His Holy Spirit. It is through prayer that we experience this new life and the power for daily living that accompanies it. And it is in prayer that our relationship with God grows and develops.

However, as our Holy Father's statement implies, our relationship with God has a purpose outside of ourselves. Made whole by His love and infused with His very life, we are to take salvation to the world. As women, our mission of salvation within the Church is to imbue the world with the aroma of Christ through an authentic living out of our femininity.

As our Blessed Lady shows us, such authenticity comes through humble obedience to the will of God. Through the power of the Holy Spirit active within us, we can surrender to the divine will with docility and obedience, following the example of the Virgin Mary, our Mother in the order of grace.

Love: The Perfect Motivation for Obedience

"Obedience" is a word that grates on the American spirit. We have inherited a nation forged in a spirit of independence, a national pride woven with self-reliance, and a culture steeped in individualism and self-determination. These national characteristics and traits have been both blessing and curse to us as a country, but to the spirit of one hoping to grow in a life of faith, they are fatal. "In Christian life obedience is something essential; it is the practical and necessary turning-point in accepting the lordship of Christ."[2]

If we are to make progress in the spiritual life, we can do so only through a spirit of obedience that lays hold of our self-will and reins it in to conform to the will of God. St. Basil says there are three dispositions of heart with which we can obey: the first is out of fear of punishment; the second is out of desire to reap a reward; the third is out of love. This third reason is the attitude of sons and daughters.[3]

As the adopted daughters of the Most High God, love is to be our motivation for obedience, just as love was the motivation that prompted the Blessed Mother's obedience at the moment of her Annunciation and kept her vigilant as she stood in the shadow of the cross on Calvary. Wanting to do God's will above all things, she said "yes" to Him and never counted the cost. "Be it done unto me according to Thy Word," she said.

Mary's *fiat* to God illustrates a great truth about obedience: it brings new life. Her obedience caused the Word to be made flesh and dwell among us (see Jn 1:14). She brought Jesus Christ into the world. And *His* obedience brought eternal life—salvation to mankind. Our obedience to God will also bring new life into our lives and into the lives of others if we say "yes" to Him without reservation.

How, then, do we obey? Just as redemptive grace forever flows from the side of Christ, providing for us in every day and age the opportunity for salvation, so too does the grace of obedience forever flow down the hill of Calvary into our lives. Obedience comes to us through the perfect source of obedience, Jesus Christ.

What we need do is take hold of the grace of obedience and use it as the reins of control that tame our self-will and bring it into submission to the will of God. Through the grace of obedience we must first root out of our will any obstacle that stands in the way of divine union and then employ positive means to strengthen the will to remain on the right path.

Obedience Enables Us to Receive God's Love

Before discussing how to purge and strengthen our self-will through the grace of obedience, it would be good for us to first define the will of God. God's ultimate will is that each of us should be restored to the state of relationship which Adam enjoyed with Him in the Garden of Eden before the Fall. This state of being was one of holy union because no stain of sin separated Adam from God.

However, when Adam disobeyed, he introduced sin into the heart of man and created a breach in man's relationship with God. Because of this first sin (original sin), man has a predisposition to sin—an inherited weakness of the will to follow his own ways rather than the ways of God. This stubbornness of heart, rooted in the will, is the source of every sin. St. Bernard says, "Take away self-will, and there will no longer be any hell."

The extent to which we are able to conform our will to the will of God is the extent to which we will begin to experience the very power of God active in our lives. And this power is first and primarily the power of love. "The aim of all is in fact to get human freedom to return freely to adhering to God, so that only one will, God's will, may reign again in the universe as was the case before sin appeared. Through obedience we have, in some way, 'the return of creatures to God.' At the head of all biblical motivations for obedience … there is charity."[4] When we obey, the love of God takes up residence within us and we become conduits of grace through which His love flows into the world, drawing all men back to Him.

What Does God Want From Us?

"'It is through obedience,' a Father of the desert said, 'that we are not only in the image of God but like to God.' We are in the image of God through the very fact of our existence, but through our obedience to Him we are like to Him, as through obedience we conform ourselves to His will and, through our free choice, become what He is by nature. We are like to God because we want what He wants."[5]

God wants us to be in loving union with Him and to be a catalyst of His love in the lives of others. Obedience is the way in which we conform to God's will, but how do we know what God's will is for us? This is a good question, for how can we aspire to be obedient unless we know what to obey?

To answer this question, let's look at the nature of God's will. In classical spirituality, there is a distinction made between God's *signified will* and His will of *good pleasure.* God's signified will constitutes the moral rudder for our lives. It is called *signified* because it clearly tells us what we must do. God's will of *good pleasure,* on the other hand, means seeing the wisdom of God in all of the providential events that take place in our lives—joyful and sorrowful—and submitting ourselves to them as a means of attaining eternal life.

In his classic *The Spiritual Life,* Adolphe Tanquerey writes: "In practice, then, conformity to God's will means doing God's will and submitting to God's will."[6] In this chapter we will look at God's signified will, and in the next chapter we will explore God's will of good pleasure.

We see an expression of the signified will of the Father in the story of the rich young man who asked Jesus, "Good Teacher, what shall I do to inherit eternal life?" (see Lk 18:18-25 and Mt 19:16-22).

Jesus replied, "You know the commandments: 'Do not commit adultery, Do not kill, Do not steal, Do not bear false witness, Honor your father and mother.'" The young man told Jesus that he had kept all of these commandments since he had been a boy. Jesus then said, "One thing you still lack. If you would be perfect, go, sell what you possess and give to the poor, and you will have treasure in heaven; and come, follow me."

We all know the end of the story. The rich young man, attached to his earthly treasure, went away sad, "for his possessions were many."

What Jesus outlines here is the signified will of the Father. We are to obey His commands *and* follow His way of love. "You shall love the Lord your God with all your heart, and with all your soul, and with all your mind, and with all your strength.... You shall love your neighbor as yourself," Jesus tells us in Mark 12:30-31. While obeying the commands of God is necessary for salvation, acting with charity leads to perfection.

St. Francis de Sales tells us,

Christian doctrine clearly proposes unto us the truths which God wills that we should believe, the goods He will have us hope for, the pains He will have us dread, what He will have us love, the commandments He will have us observe and the counsels He desires us to follow. And this is called God's signified will, because He has signified and made manifest unto us that it is His will and intention that all this should be believed, hoped for, feared, loved, and practiced.[7]

The signified will of God, then, requires obedience in three main areas:

- Obedience to the commandments of God and the precepts of the Church
- Obedience to the evangelical counsels of poverty, chastity, and obedience in conformity with our state in life
- Obedience to the inspirations of grace, also called the promptings of the Holy Spirit.

To be in God's will, this is the minimum we should do. Let's take a look at each area and see how it applies to us in our lives.

Obedience to the Commands of God
and the Precepts of the Church

When we are seeking the will of God in our lives in general or in a particular situation, we must first determine if we are in full obedience to the commandments of God. He has given us the Ten Commandments not to diminish our freedom, but rather to increase it.

By fulfilling the Commandments, we ensure that we are not being held in bondage to sin. Thus, we can fully appreciate the abundant life God desires for us. As beings with rational minds, we are proficient in justifying our behavior. Illicit relationships, harmful habits, sinful ways can all be legitimized by our minds, which are weakened through sin. The Ten Commandments are our insurance policy. If we strive to be faithful to them, we are assured of being in the will of the Father.

It is as we work to fulfill the commands of God through obedience to them that we begin to purge our self-will. Reminding us that our Baptism in Christ has made us a new creation, St. Paul tells us: "Put off your old nature which belongs to your former manner of life and is corrupt through deceitful lusts, and be renewed in the Spirit of your minds" (Eph 4:22).

What is this former way of life, the old self, that deteriorates through illusion and desire? It is any singular action or pattern of behavior that is rooted in sin—"evil thoughts, fornication, theft, murder, adultery, coveting, wickedness, deceit, licentiousness, envy, slander, pride, foolishness" (Mk 7:21-22). It includes immorality, obscene and suggestive talk, fornication, idolatry, anger, wrath, malice, foul language and lying, insincerity, and guile (see Eph 5:3-15; Col 3:5-11; 1 Pt 2:1-3). Anything that is in opposition to the commandments of God and the Beatitudes of Christ is sin; it creates a breach in our relationship with God, thereby prohibiting us from conforming to His will.

By following the Ten Commandments and using Scripture as our moral compass, we make great progress in finding and following the signified will of God. And yet, God has provided another invaluable source of guidance and direction: the teachings of the Roman Catholic Church. Led by the Holy Spirit, the Magisterium of Holy Mother Church gives us wisdom and insight regarding those matters that face us in our life with God. She points out heresy and false teaching, abuses and excesses, ethical concerns and human rights considerations. She instructs us through preaching the Word of God, interpreting Sacred Scripture, and giving us catechetical education. In all cases, by adhering to her teaching, we can be confident we are conforming to God's will.

This means, of course, that we have a responsibility to both know what the Church has to say in these areas and then apply her teachings to our lives. Does my position on contraception, sterilization, and birth control agree with Church teaching? If not, I need to adjust my perspective. What is my attitude toward abortion, euthanasia, and doctor-assisted suicide? Does it line up with the teachings of the Church? If not, I need to adjust my perspective. As an employer, do I comply with the Holy Father's teaching about social justice in areas regarding my employees, their wages, their family needs? No? Then I need to adjust my perspective.

And still, there is more we need to consider. We must acknowledge the fact that many aspects of our current culture, its institutions, and its media are permeated with secularism and ethical relativism. We must examine ourselves according to the teachings of the Church and the commandments of God to see to what extent we have grown lax.

Writing in his apostolic letter *Tertio Millennio Adveniente* (On the Coming Third Millennium), Pope John Paul II tells us that the sons and daughters of the Church must ask themselves a serious question: "To what extent have they been shaped by the climate of secularism and ethical relativism? And what responsibility do they bear, in view of the increasing lack of religion, for not having shown the true face of God, by having 'failed in their religious, moral, or social life?'"[8]

This is a difficult question, and one that requires integrity of heart and spirit if we are to answer it honestly. We must pray for the light of the Holy Spirit, so we may see these areas. And we must pray for the grace of obedience so that we may root these areas out of our lives. In all cases, we must be brutally honest with ourselves so that no spot, blemish, or stain remains on the windows of our soul through our own neglect, stubbornness, or pride.

The Way to Triple Harmony With God: Poverty, Chastity, and Obedience

Prior to the Fall, Adam (who was unencumbered by sin) enjoyed holy union with God. At that time, complete and total harmony existed between God's will and man's will. We read in Genesis that Adam and God conversed familiarly and walked in the cool of the night together.

The profound nature of this divine union between Adam and God was effective in producing harmony in two other areas as well. Because Adam had not yet sinned, no conflict existed between his bodily appetites and the soul. Since the soul was perfectly surrendered to God, it controlled the passions and desires of the senses which were subject to the reason and will. Thus, Adam was in harmony within himself. And this interior harmony within Adam was the source of an exterior harmony between Adam and the rest of creation.

Because the soul had power over Adam's sensual appetites, there was harmony between the body and exterior goods. Adam had stewardship over the things of the earth, dominion over all creation. Because no inordinate desire in Adam caused him to abuse or overindulge in the things of the world, creation on its part functioned accordingly—the animals were docile and the earth produced fruit without the "sweat of the brow." This three-fold harmony—between God and man, between man's soul and man's body, and between the body and exterior goods—is called *the triple harmony* in classical spirituality.[9]

However, man disrupted this harmony by revolting against the highest of the three—his union with God—and thus introduced conflict and disorder into all of the areas in which he had previously enjoyed union. Instead, three moral wounds now rule over man's heart and mind.[10] St. John describes these as carnal allurements (desire of the flesh), enticements of the eye (the desire of the eyes), and the life of empty show (the pride in riches) (see 1 Jn 2:16).

"I will not serve" has become the battle cry of the human heart. And this stance of disobedience is responsible not only for man's personal disorder but for the disorder which exists between individuals and nations and between man and the rest of creation. Out of union with God and no longer functioning in the light of truth, the soul creates its own moral standards, false and dark, with a sense of reality that is skewed and broken. Proudly determined, the body refuses to submit to the authority of God and turns a deaf ear to the voice of reason and the influence of the will. Thus, it succumbs to the passions of the flesh and the appetites of the senses. Finally, the body becomes the slave of desire for exterior goods. A lust for riches, material goods, comforts, and luxury overtakes the human heart, a quest that often leads to further sin but always leads to disillusionment, dissatisfaction, and displeasure.

These three moral wounds lead to attachment to the things of earth rather than the things of God. It was in these areas that the rich young man struggled with Jesus' proposition: "If you seek perfection, sell all you have and give to the poor. You will have treasure in heaven. Then come and follow me." The rich young man, attached to his status and position, to his earthly treasure and all that it bought him, was unable to respond to Jesus' invitation. He went away sad, *"for his possessions were many."* In calling him to give up those attachments, Jesus was asking him to return to that triple harmony which existed in the Garden of Eden before the Fall. And it is to this harmony that Jesus invites each one of us as well.

A personal experience with attachment. As I have shared earlier, my recommitment to God came at a point in my life when I was disillusioned. Externally, all looked well. My husband loved me, my children were beautiful and healthy, and we were financially secure, enjoying the pleasures that money could buy. But internally, I was a mess. My life was disordered. Not only was I attached to the things of the world, but in several areas I was in bondage. I didn't recognize how enslaved I had become to the appetites of the senses until the Lord gently began to point them out to me, one by one. Some of these were easier to overcome than others, and some of them may only be brought into complete submission in purgatory, but overcoming one of them made a lasting impression on me.

It was Ash Wednesday, and a beautiful spring day in sunny Florida. I was on my lunch hour, driving up State Road 580 toward my favorite destination—the shopping mall. Shopping was my passion. In fact, I had to make at least one trip a day to the store and buy something—anything, it didn't matter. We had an attorney friend at the time who used to tell me I was the world's ultimate consumer—and I took it as a compliment!

On this particular spring afternoon, I had turned on the radio to my favorite Christian station. The windows were down, my left arm was in the air praising the Lord, and I was singing at the top of my lungs. As the song came to an end, I began to tell the Lord how much I loved Him. I told Him I would do anything for Him. Over and over again I sang out my gratefulness for His mercy and love, for His Passion and death, for His resurrection. I thanked Him for loving me so much that He gave His life for me, and for having brought me back into relationship with Him. I told Him that all I desired was a deeper union with Him, and I asked Him to remove from me anything that stood in the way of that union. Little did I know how literally He would take those words!

I arrived at the mall and pulled into a parking space very close to one of the main entrances. I whispered a quick "thank You" to God for providing me with such an ideal space, put the car in park, and turned off the ignition. Quietly, deep within my spirit, I sensed a voice saying, "Johnnette, do you really love Me?"

I recognized this as the Lord's voice, talking with me in my heart. "Yes, Lord. You know I love You. Haven't I been telling You this my whole way to the mall?"

"Johnnette, if you love Me," the voice said, "then don't go shopping today."

"Don't go shopping!" I cried. "This can't be so. It's Ash Wednesday, Lord, and I saw a dress yesterday that I'd like to have for Easter. I was just going in to get it."

"Johnnette," the voice continued, "you said you'd do anything for me. Would you please not go shopping today?"

"Oh, Lord, I didn't know You'd ask me not to shop. I thought maybe You'd call me to the mission field or something. But, not shop—I don't know if I can do that!" I lamented.

"Johnnette, I'd like you to give up shopping for Lent," He persisted.

"For Lent!" I cried. "Lent is forty days, Lord—and it's only Ash Wednesday! How on earth could I do this for Lent? What about my Easter dress?"

"Johnnette, you can't do this on your own, but through My grace all things are possible."

What could I say? Jesus was holding me to my word. I had promised Him I would do anything for Him. And I had asked Him to remove from me anything which was a hindrance to my union with Him. Though I had not seen it before, I was beginning to suspect that shopping had become an addiction for me, an attachment that came dangerously close to idolatry. I knew Jesus was offering me the grace in that moment to overcome this bondage in my life. He was offering me the opportunity to return to Him a part of myself that had been closed off to Him through attachment to worldly things. And if I agreed, He would heal me of this lust for possessions and material goods. In that moment, I understood that my passion for shopping was a feeble attempt to fill up a hole in my heart that could only be filled with the presence of God.

"Lord," I responded, "I can only tell You that this is going to be difficult. But, if You give me the grace, I will try to be faithful to Your request. However, at the moment I'm really having a hard time even turning on the car to leave."

"I'm giving you the grace," I sensed the Lord say. "Just turn the key in the ignition, put the car in reverse, and go back to the office. The grace is there. Use it."

With that, I turned on the car, backed out of the space, and headed to the office. As I walked in the front door of the building, I was elated. "You did it, Lord," I cried. "I made it back without so much as buying a pack of chewing gum! This is great."

"Johnnette, thank you for using the grace I offered you," I seemed to hear the Lord say. And my eyes filled with tears at the profound mystery of God's action in my life.

I cannot tell you that I wasn't tempted throughout that Lent to go shopping. I was tempted. At times, sorely so. However, God in

His goodness continued to give me the grace to resist. And by the time Easter Sunday came, both my need to shop and my desire to shop were gone. Jesus had healed me by filling that empty space in my heart with His own loving presence.

God wants to heal us of every inordinate attachment so that we might be completely filled with Him.

Balm for the wounded soul: the practice of detachment. The spiritual antidote for the three moral wounds to the soul are the three evangelical counsels—poverty, chastity, and obedience. By practicing them, the triple harmony is restored to our lives. Through interior poverty we enter into right relationship with God. Through chastity our soul controls our bodily appetites. And through obedience our selfish wants and desires give way to prudent stewardship over the things of the world. Through the counsels a spirit of detachment to worldly wants and desires is formed so that the heart is free to grow in holiness.

For men and women who are called to religious life, these three counsels take the form of promises and vows through which the individual offers his or her life to God as an oblation or sacrifice. The counsels are practiced by restraint in the ownership of material possessions, through a vow of chastity which includes celibacy, and by obedience to God and to the authority of superiors.

It is not practical for the lay person to live out the evangelical counsels in the same way as those who have been called to the religious life. However, the laity is still called to the *spirit of detachment* which the counsels engender. God asks us to value human life above material wealth, the human person above comfort and luxury, the kingdom of God above the desires of the flesh, the will of God above convenience and selfish wants. We must mortify our senses by guarding our eyes and ears, guarding the inner recesses of our hearts from anything which would take precedence over our love of God or compromise our ability to obey Him in love.

How to cultivate a spirit of detachment. To cultivate a spirit of detachment, we should critically appraise our wants and desires, our thoughts and our deeds, in light of the Holy Spirit and God's holy will. Asking some hard questions will encourage us to let go of those things that are spiritually harmful and cling to those things that will help us to deepen our relationship with God.

1. *Is there anything to which I have an inordinate attachment?* What is my attitude toward my job or career? Toward food and drink? Toward gambling and shopping, housecleaning and social functions? Has ministry itself become an idol—that is, has it taken God's place as my highest priority?

2. *Do I practice charity through tithing, almsgiving, and generosity with my time and talent?* Do I spend some time in volunteer work, freely giving of my gifts and abilities to build up the kingdom of God through service? Do I give of my treasure to those who need it—organizations or individuals? When I give, is my attitude one of cheerfulness and gratitude, or is it grudging?

3. *Do the things I take in through my senses lead me closer to God or away from Him?* What do I watch on television? What do I read? What kind of movies do I attend? How do I spend my free time? Do I have a problem with pornography? Do I dress modestly? Am I involved in any immoral relationships? Is my marriage a chaste one?

4. *How do I stand on the issue of obedience?* Do I accept what I am told to do by employers, heads of committees, my parish priest, my spouse, as commands coming from God Himself—to the extent that their orders do not conflict with God's standards? Do I respond with openness of heart or with grumbling? Do I

look for God's will when making important decisions in my life, or do I rush ahead with my own plans? Do I practice docility of spirit, or am I quick to fight for my own way?

If we honestly strive to cultivate a spirit of detachment through the observance of the evangelical counsels, we will make real spiritual progress as we seek union with the divine will. Father Tanquerey tells us, "The more generous we are in giving ourselves over to the practice of the counsels compatible with the duties of our state, the closer we draw unto Our Lord, for such counsels are the expression of His designs upon us."[11]

Obedience to Inspirations of Grace and the Promptings of the Holy Spirit

Our call as women is to live out our femininity authentically, to *"aid humanity in not falling,"* and in so doing to become the healers of the world. To accomplish this mission through us, God often gives us inspirations, promptings, and interior urges that encourage us toward charitable acts or apostolic works. Occasionally, He will inspire us to do an extraordinary act of service in His name. When we heed these promptings, they become moments of grace for us and others.

Recall the Blessed Virgin Mary's visit to her cousin, Elizabeth. Prompted by God through the angel's announcement that Elizabeth was with child in her old age, Mary journeyed to her cousin's home to be of service to her. Through obedience to the Word of God, Mary became a blessing not only to her cousin, but also to the child in Elizabeth's womb.

As we determine to live out our lives in obedience to the will of the Father, then, it becomes apparent that we must choose to obey Him in all things, including these inspirations of grace and promptings of the Holy Spirit. However, it is important for us to discern the origin and cause of an idea or thought, lest we be the victim of our own enthusiasm, passion, or imagination—or, worse yet, a delusion of the Evil One. How, then, do we know if a prompting is from God?

Generally speaking, if the prompting conforms with the ordinary acts of charity for people in our state of life who are attempting to live a life of holiness, and if there is nothing immoral or questionable about the action, we should carry it out with gratitude that God has asked us to serve Him in this way. If, however, the prompting is out of the ordinary and is potentially life-changing in scope, we should put it to the test by evaluating it against several criteria.

1. *First of all, is it fully in line with Sacred Scripture, the Ten Commandments, and the teachings of the Church?* There is no contradiction in God—He will never go against His own precepts. If a particular action is in opposition to Sacred Scripture, it is not of God. If it goes against one of the Commandments, it is not of God. If it opposes a teaching of the Church, it is not of God. If it is an uncharitable act, it is not of God. If it opposes the natural law, it is not of God. If it violates *legitimate* civil authority, it is not of God.

2. *Second, is the prompting proceeding from virtue or the flesh?* Another way to ask this question is, "What is my motivation?" If the desire flows from selfish gain, pride, or ostentation, the chances are very good that this is a prompting from the flesh rather than from the Spirit of God. However, if we can honestly answer that the motivation stems from the virtue of charity and love of God, then we can feel safe that our intention is honorable.

3. *Third, has this prompting been confirmed in other ways?* God wants us to be assured of His call. He does not want us to suffer

from confusion, dismay, or uncertainty. Therefore, He confirms His will for us in a variety of ways. Often, the very prompting we are experiencing will be suggested to us by someone else. Occasionally, someone will speak the words to us directly. And at other times, through the normal course of conversation, a homily at Mass, a comment on the radio or television, we will recognize God's voice. God also uses Scripture to confirm His word to us. In reading a passage, the words will seem to jump off the page or they will burn in our hearts long after we close the Bible. Still another way that God speaks to us is through the events of the day. Occurrences happen that seem to fit perfectly with the word we are receiving in our hearts.

4. *Has the prompting withstood the test of time?* Sometimes our enthusiasm pushes us to a decision before we have taken the time to adequately evaluate it. However, God does not take away His will for us. If we have sensed an inspiration for some time and it is valid in all other areas, we should take the prompting seriously. A spiritual director once told me that there is a world of difference between enthusiasm and zeal. Enthusiasm is rooted in the emotions, while zeal is rooted in the Spirit. We must give ourselves the time we need to allow our enthusiasm to turn to zeal, for only then will it be a conduit of grace in the lives of others.

5. *Am I going through an emotionally difficult time, or am I suffering from mental instability?* If I am going through a difficult time emotionally—because of a serious illness, the death of a loved one, a serious financial reversal, a separation or divorce, a major disappointment or setback—or if I am suffering a mental illness or disorder that is not being treated, it is unlikely that the prompting I am hearing is coming from God. God's desire for us at times like these is usually that we be healed by Him

through others—doctors, pastors, counselors, spiritual directors. All major decisions should be delayed, if at all possible, until we are well. This applies to ministry as well. It is a time for us to be ministered to, rather than a time to be active in ministry.

6. *Have I sought the counsel of others?* Few people are in a position to make major decisions on their own; even if a person *is* in this position, it is not usually wise. For those in religious life, the guidance and permission of superiors, provincials, or bishops must be sought and obtained. Those who are married must reach agreement with their spouses, carefully considering the effects of the decision on family members. However, God often asks us to make sacrifices, and the appearance of a sacrifice should not be cause for a negative decision.

Spiritual direction is absolutely necessary when making life-changing decisions, although we should be able to judge ordinary promptings by the above criteria.

7. *Is the supposed prompting or inspiration of grace in conformity with my state in life?* We must weigh the promptings we receive against our state in life. If we sense that God is asking us to participate in certain activities, go into a particular ministry, or become a member of a certain apostolate, it will not take away from the obligations of our life in other areas. There may be sacrifice, as previously mentioned, but there will not be conflict. If there is, we must scrutinize the inspiration more closely. If the prompting is of God and there appears to be an obstacle or block, our attitude of heart has to be one of patient endurance—all will come to pass in His time.

Once we determine that a prompting is from the Holy Spirit and a legitimate inspiration of grace, then we need to heed it with faith and confidence, knowing that God is directing us and leading us and that "he who began a good work in you will bring it to completion at the day of Jesus Christ" (Phil 1:6). And often, when we heed the prompting that God is giving us, it becomes a moment of grace and conversion in our lives as well as in the lives of others.

I had an experience that illustrates how necessary it is to heed the promptings of the Holy Spirit. After coming into a deeper relationship with Jesus Christ, my thirst for Sacred Scripture was insatiable. So much did I love the Word of God that I wanted to read it in a variety of translations and paraphrases. One day I decided to purchase a copy of a particular translation at a local Christian bookstore. Since the bookstore was not a Catholic one, there was no Catholic edition in stock. But the clerk told me she would be happy to order it for me.

I gave her my name and daytime telephone number, and didn't think about it any more until the phone rang at work one afternoon. It was the clerk at the bookstore calling to tell me my Bible had arrived. It had taken much longer to come in than I had expected, so I was pleased to receive her call.

As soon as I could break away from the office, I went to the bookstore to pick up my new Bible. I pulled into the parking space, hurried into the store, approached the sales counter, and told the clerk why I was there. She handed me a beautiful green hardback Bible edged in gold. This was much finer than the edition I had in mind. "But gee, it's lovely," I thought. I looked down and to my surprise, it said, *Die Heilige Bibel*. The Bible was in German!

"Ma'am," I said, "there must be some mistake. I ordered a *Catholic* edition of this Bible, not a *German* one."

"No, Mrs. Benkovic. This is what you ordered. I have your request right here. See? It says '*German Bible. Quantity - One.*'"

"Ma'am, I don't understand how this could have happened. I wouldn't have ordered a German Bible. I don't speak German—much less read it."

"Well, I'm sorry. This was a special order, as you might imagine. That's why it took so long to come in. And your request says this is what you ordered."

Frankly, I couldn't imagine how this mix-up had occurred. I was very clear in what I requested the day I ordered the Bible. I watched the woman take the order. Did something different come out of my mouth than what I was thinking? Could I have spoken one thing and the clerk have heard something else? I didn't know. But I do know that sometimes the Holy Spirit allows circumstances to occur for reasons far beyond our comprehension.

What is He asking me to do in this instance? I wondered. Though I had no answer for this question, I decided to purchase the Bible anyway.

"Wrap it up. I'll take it," I told the salesclerk.

I put the German Bible in the backseat of my car and I drove around with it for months. Each time it caught my eye I would ask our Lord to let me know what I was to do with it at the appropriate time.

One afternoon He answered my prayer. On my way home from work, I decided to stop at a little shop I had often noticed but never visited. It featured a variety of items for home decorating, and its brightly colored window displays often caught my eye. I entered the store, anticipating some lovely moments of browsing. It was late in the day and only a few customers were in the store. I was there only a few moments when a large blonde woman approached me. "May I help you?" she asked in a decidedly German accent. Instantly, I knew the German Bible was meant for her. My heart began to beat wildly; now that I was actually seeing the person who was meant to receive the Bible, I was a bit nervous. I never figured I'd be offering it to someone in a public place.

"Lord," I prayed, "are you sure she's the one to get this Bible? What if she throws me out of the store? There are other people in here, Lord. This doesn't seem like a very good time to evangelize. What if she isn't happy about it or doesn't like what I say? I don't want to offend her, Lord."

"She's the one, Johnnette," I sensed the Lord say.

"Ma'am," the German saleswoman said again, this time a bit testily, "may I help you?"

"Yes, you may," I sputtered. "But before you do, I have something I'd like to give you," I said as I backed my way to the door. "I'll be right back." The German woman looked at me strangely, and I could feel her eyes following me the entire walk to my car. My heart was beating furiously.

"Lord," I complained, "this woman doesn't seem very friendly. And I think I've upset her. I'll bet she thinks I'm crazy. I'll be lucky if she doesn't call the police. Give me the right words to say, Lord. Please prepare her heart to receive this Bible!"

As I reentered the store, the German woman raised her painted eyebrows at me. She wasn't smiling. "I'd better do this fast," I thought, "or I won't do it at all."

"Ma'am," I began as if this were an everyday occurrence, "I just happened to have this German Bible in the backseat of my car, and since you have a German accent you must be German, and I thought you might like to have it. Here, it's yours." With that, I handed her the Bible. She took it, glanced at it, looked at me, screamed, and ran into the back room. I was mortified. What had I done?

"This is not the reaction I expected, Lord," I lamented. "What is going on?" The few customers who were in the store turned and looked at me long and hard. Their consternation froze me in place. Within seconds a young man peered around the corner of the back room and motioned for me to come. All kinds of thoughts raced through my head. *What if the lady screams again? What should I say? Who is this young man and why do they want me in the back room?*

I considered my options. I could make a run for the front door or I could see this thing through. I decided on the latter. Mustering up what little dignity I had left, I followed the young man's motion and slipped around the corner into the back room.

There, at a little table, sat the large blonde German woman. Her ample size dwarfed her surroundings, and yet there was something tiny and frail about her as she sat there. She told me to sit. I sat. The young man—her son—sat, too.

"Why did you bring me this book?" she asked as her index finger thumped the green leather cover of the German Bible.

My heart was in my throat. "Well, like I told you, I just happened to have this German Bible in my car and I thought you would like to have it. That's all."

She raised one eyebrow as she closed the opposite eye. "How did you know?" she asked.

What was she talking about? I wondered. I didn't *know* anything. Aloud I said, "I'm sure I don't know what you mean."

"A few days ago I found out that my business partner embezzled the money from this business. I'm bankrupt. Broke. Last night I made a decision. I decided to take matters into my own hands. I'll take care of him, *my* way," she said as she clenched her fist.

I couldn't believe what I was hearing, and I hoped my face didn't register my shock. I could feel my temples pulsate. She continued, "Today, I began to plot just what I would do. And now, you come. And you bring me this!" She thumped the Bible once again. I was beginning to get a clear picture of just how she intended to take things into her own hands.

Somewhere I heard my voice speaking. Amazingly, it sounded confident. "Your plans are not the solution to your problems," I said. "I'm sure God wants you to work this out some other way."

Fatigue moved across this lady's face as storm clouds rush in on a summer's afternoon. The weight of her burden was finally taking its toll on her. "We'll see, we'll see," she said. Lifting the Bible, she said again, "I'll read this and we'll see."

I gave her my card and told her to call me if she wanted to talk. A few days later she did call. She told me that she had begun to read the psalms and they were bringing her great comfort. She also told me that a Lutheran minister, new to the area, called her home by accident one night. They began a conversation and she had put aside her plans of malice. She thanked me for giving her the Bible. She received it at a critical moment, she said, and she knew God was in the midst of it.

As I hung up the telephone, I could only marvel at the power and mystery of God. He knew months in advance how this Bible would be used. He knew exactly the moment that woman would be open to receiving it. And He knew precisely the impact it would have on her. And *I* knew that if it wasn't for His grace, I could never have given it to her.

God only asks that we heed His promptings, for every act of obedience to Him brings new life. When we choose to obey, through the grace of God, we reflect His love to the world. You and I are called to be givers of life by doing the will of God. We know that there is no lasting happiness apart from this. Created in His image and likeness, we long to cooperate with His grace so that His Image may be perfected in us.

Through the gift of His Holy Spirit and submission to His signified will, the Divine Life takes up residence within us, and we come to an infused knowledge of God and His ways. This is the gift of wisdom. In our next chapter we will explore this gift of the Holy Spirit and how it interacts with yet another aspect of God's will, His will of *good pleasure*. May we, in peace and gratitude, continue on the road to holiness, encouraged as always by the communion of saints, especially Mary, our Mother in the order of grace.

FIVE

Wisdom: Vision for the Abundant Life

*T*he spiritual life is a cooperative venture between God and man. Out of His love for us, God gives us the grace to live out His holy will. And in response to that love, we accept, receive, and act upon that grace. The extent to which we respond to God's initiative of grace is the extent to which we make progress in the spiritual life. As we grow in holiness, we begin to obtain a certain knowledge of God through which we gain understanding of Him and His action in our lives and in the world around us.

Seeing the world and our place in it through the light of this knowledge is a manifestation of wisdom, a gift of the Holy Spirit. Wisdom "is a knowledge not learned from books but given by God who illumines and fills our mind and heart, will and understanding with love. By means of this light of love, the Christian has a more intimate and joyful knowledge of God and his mysteries."[1] Wisdom, then, is the fruit of love—God's love for us which we in turn accept and act upon.

As we discussed in the last chapter, we respond to God's love by obedience to His *signified* will. Initially, our obedience to God's signified will might be motivated by a sense of obligation, duty, or fear. But, as we continue to grow in holiness, the impetus for our obedience changes from one of necessity to one of love, a desire to please the Beloved. Through this movement of heart, we dispose ourselves to receive the gift of wisdom, and as we faithfully continue to obey God's will, a holy perspective of life develops within us. The eyes of our soul, once clouded by the cataracts of sin, self-will, and lust for personal possessions, riches, or honors, are now able to see the events and circumstances of daily life with true clarity and vision.

As the Divine Life takes up residence within us, we see the world from God's perspective, and we find that everything in life is laden with supernatural value. We see that the silver and gold threads of God's grace weave the fabric of our lives and the tapestry of the world, making all creation shimmer with His holy presence. In short, our vision of the world changes from a purely sensate or natural perspective—one that is centered on self—to one that is informed by the knowledge and understanding of God—one that is centered on divine love. This "intimate and joyful knowledge of God and his mysteries," which we call *wisdom,* springs from loving conformity to the will of God.

Wisdom in Troubled Times

Wisdom, the ability to see the hand of God at work in and through all circumstances, transforms our perspective. Through the gift of wisdom, we can rejoice in the midst of trial, be prudent in the midst of joy, and be zealous in the midst of the mundane because we are infused with the understanding and knowledge of God. All events and situations can be appraised from this vantage point, and this yields a life influenced by good judgment and sound decision.

The gift of wisdom ... enables the soul to taste the goodness of God, to see it manifested in all events, even in the most painful, since God permits evil only for a higher good.... The gift of wisdom thus makes us judge everything in relation to God.... It reminds us that all that glitters is not gold and that, on the contrary, marvels of grace are to be found under the humblest exteriors.[2]

God desires that His children come to see all of creation—the world and its events, their individual lives, circumstances, and situations—from His perspective. Only through this vision of life will we be able to experience the fullness of God's love for us and His abiding presence in and through all things.

However, when we struggle with problems, trials, tribulations, and heartaches, our vision can be clouded and the will of God obscured. In these moments, those silver and gold threads of God's grace appear tarnished, dull, and lifeless. Indeed, we may wonder whether God is present at all, for the circumstances speak of absence, not presence; frustration, not peace; betrayal, not support; abandonment, not love.

But even when life overwhelms us, God's grace is with us still. His wisdom is always available to us. All we need do is cooperate with His grace through obedience. It is in these moments that God asks us to be submissive to His will of *good pleasure,* sometimes called His *permissive will.*

God's Will of Good Pleasure

God's will of good pleasure is "the ruling principle that *governs* all things with wisdom, directing the course of events so as to make them work together unto His glory and the salvation of men."[3]

In moments of trial and discouragement, we cooperate with God's will of good pleasure by investing into the circumstance or situation the absolute certainty that our God loves us and that any action He permits in our lives is meant for our ultimate good and sanctification. Thus, we conform to God's permissive will.

This conformity "rests upon this basis, that nothing happens without God's order or permission, and that God, being infinite Perfection and infinite Goodness, cannot will or permit anything but for the good of the souls He has created, although this is not always apparent to our eyes."[4] Submitting to God's will of good pleasure calls forth from us all that we have learned of trust, all that we have learned of faith, and all that we have learned of hope. Thus, this submission brings us to spiritual maturity.

Cultivating Wisdom in the Garden of the Soul: Three Stages to Christian Perfection

St. Bernard distinguishes three degrees of conformity to the will of God, which correspond to the three stages of Christian perfection: "The beginner, moved by fear, patiently bears the Cross of Christ; the one who has already made some progress on the road to perfection, inspired by hope, carries it cheerfully; the perfect soul, consumed by love, embraces it ardently."[5]

Following this same line of thinking, Louis Colin, C.SS.R., writes this about submission to God's will: "Active conformity: to do all that God wants us to do—that is obedience. Passive conformity: to suffer all that God wills us to suffer—that is patience. Conformity of total surrender: to cast ourselves into the Arms of God and let Him act—that is abandonment to Providence. These three terms express the perfect union of our will with that of God."[6]

In moments of trial, we are called to "conformity of total surrender" as we ardently embrace our suffering and cast ourselves with complete abandon into God's arms of love. This is submission to God's permissive will, a submission not marked by resignation or futility, but rather, a proactive submission that is undergirded with faith, reinforced with trust, informed by the knowledge and wisdom that "all things work for good for those who love God, who are called according to his purpose" (Rom 8:28, NAB).

As we have mentioned, the spiritual life requires our cooperation with the grace God gives us. Therefore, though wisdom is a gift of the Holy Spirit, there is much we can do to dispose ourselves to receive it.

This process of readying our hearts to receive wisdom might be compared to the efforts we make in cultivating a garden. First, we "prepare the land." Just as we diligently remove all weeds from the plot of soil, so too do we weed our heart from any tendencies and attitudes that do not glorify God. This "weeding" is done through obedience to the laws of God and His Church. Next, we till the soil, making it ready to receive the seed. By pursuing the evangelical counsels and acting upon inspirations of grace, the soil of our heart is softened and made receptive.

Then, we plant the seeds we need to produce the desired fruit. To yield the fruit of wisdom, we plant the seed of renewal, the seed of virtue, and the seed of holy reflection. These three seeds produce fruit in abundance.

Finally, we water our garden with the soaking rain of spiritual direction. This sweet rain of grace encourages the seedlings to grow roots—strong and deep—in the rich soil of truth. Thus does our garden produce a good and nourishing fruit that grows to maturity and can be shared with others.

The Seed of Renewal—Renewing the Mind According to God's Standard

In St. Paul's letter to the Romans we read, "Do not be conformed to this world but be transformed by the renewal of your mind, that you may prove what is the will of God, what is good and accept-able and perfect" (Rom 12:2). To some extent, all of us have been shaped by the prevailing culture. However, in this passage, St. Paul calls us to a higher ideal, a greater standard. He tells us that we must not conform ourselves to the current of popular opinion, but rather we must renew our minds. Only through a mind renewed according to the standards of God can we judge what is His will, what is the good in each situation, what is pleasing to God in each circumstance, and what will lead us to our ultimate goal—the per-fection of Christian charity. Only as women who are renewed according to the standards of God will we be able to accomplish our mission, our divine "munus" of *"aiding humanity in not falling"* and becoming healers in the world.

Not long ago my husband and I were talking about the differ-ences between information, knowledge, and the wisdom of God. Through the wonders of modern technology, we can obtain infor-mation from any part of the world within a matter of seconds. Any number of diverse facts and data can be ours in the time it takes to dial a telephone number and click a button. But this doesn't make us an intelligent culture, or even a knowledgeable culture. In order for information to be useful, it must come together to form a body of knowledge. Otherwise, it remains only data and isolated facts, yielding no cohesive perspective about a subject, category, or area of discipline.

Through in-depth study in a particular area—medicine, engi-neering, theology, carpentry—we acquire knowledge. Our infor-mation has come together to form a body of knowledge that becomes useful to ourselves and others. However, though we may be a proficient scholar, a brilliant academic, though we may gradu-ate summa cum laude, attain honors and distinctions, be given accolades and awarded prizes, wisdom may escape us still.

For wisdom is not about facts and data, not about information nor ideas, not about knowledge and accomplishment; rather, wisdom is a view of the world which has been infused with the very mind of God. It is seeing all things through the eyes of Eternal Wisdom. It is acquiring a godly perspective of the world, our place in it, and the events and circumstances that impact our lives. To attain wisdom, we must heed St. Paul's advice and set about the business of renewing our minds through the guidance and direction of the Holy Spirit.

In the previous chapter, we talked about the need to detach from the things of the world so that we might be free to aspire to the things of God. As we begin to free ourselves from patterns of behavior, excessive wants and desires for material things, and attitudes of heart and mind which have maintained a premier position within us, we must begin to put in their place activities and practices, thoughts and ideas, aspirations and desires which lead us in the direction of God's will. In this way, our minds will be renewed and we will be transformed (see Rom 12:2). Following are some of the essential holy practices that help us acquire wisdom.

The Sacrament of Reconciliation

The prayerful reception of the Sacrament of Reconciliation is essential if we are to keep a close watch over the condition of our souls. We must receive the sacrament with integrity—being honest with ourselves and being honest with God through His priest—if we are to reap the spiritual benefits of this occasion of grace. We must go to the sacrament prepared to encounter the merciful heart of Jesus, to be washed clean by the power of redemptive grace, and to be invigorated with new life. The Sacrament of Reconciliation is also a healing sacrament, capable of cauterizing the wounds of our hearts which cause us pain and keep us from experiencing God's divine love for us.

The Sacrament of the Eucharist

If we are to renew our minds, we must come to the eucharistic table fully recollected and aware of the One whom we are about to receive. Jesus Christ is fully present in the Sacred Host—body and blood, soul and divinity. And He has seen fit, in the utmost act of humility, to entrust Himself to our hands, to our lips, to our hearts. It is through the Eucharistic Presence that Jesus remains with us until the end of time, and our hearts should tremble with holy awe as we consider the supreme privilege which we are offered. (We will be discussing this most holy of sacraments more fully in the next chapter.)

Renewing the Mind Through Personal Prayer

It is through a regular and consistent prayer time that we truly experience the transforming power of a relationship with God.

Prayer must be the backbone of our spiritual life. It supplies the form and shape for all that takes place within us. In our time of prayer, our whole being—heart, mind, and will—must be prepared to meet God for an intimate moment of holy conversation, fully receptive to whatever inspiration or grace, word or directive He may give us. But mostly, we come to our time of prayer as we would come to meet our Beloved—ready to just spend time with Him, gazing into His eyes of love.

The Holy Activity of Spiritual Reading and Study

Of course, spiritual reading and study includes Sacred Scripture, which maintains the position of priority, but our reading should also include the lives of the saints, books written by the saints, and contemporary literature that offers an authentic approach to following God.

We must also include the *Catechism of the Catholic Church* and the encyclicals, letters, and writings of our Holy Father. Such holy reading incites our mind with inspiration and truth while it fills our hearts with desire for the things of God.

Seeking Opportunities for Growth Within the Faith Community

Participating in religious services, as well as attending conferences and retreats that uphold an authentically Catholic experience of God, helps us to grow strong in our walk of faith.

Again, the disposition of our heart is essential when engaging in these activities. We must come with a heart that is teachable, one that seeks to be conformed to the will of God. We must also come with expectant faith, believing that God, in His love for us, will make His holy will known to us.

In all of these ways we begin to comply with the instruction that St. Paul gives to the Romans to transform our minds. By proactively renewing our minds with the things of God, we begin to find that worldly knowledge gives way to supernatural understanding, conventional understanding gives way to godly wisdom, and human wisdom gives way to spiritual judgment. St. Paul put it this way to the Corinthians:

> *Yet among the mature we do impart wisdom, although it is not a wisdom of this age or of the rulers of this age, who are doomed to pass away. But we impart a secret and hidden wisdom of God…. And we impart this in words not taught by human wisdom but taught by the Spirit, interpreting spiritual truths to those who possess the Spirit. The unspiritual man does not receive the gifts of the Spirit of God, for they are folly to him, and he is not able to understand them because they are spiritually discerned. The spiritual man judges all things, but is himself to be judged by no one. "For who has known the mind of the Lord so as to instruct him?" But we have the mind of Christ.*
>
> 1 CORINTHIANS 2:6-7, 13-16

Paul is not advocating a judgmental, self-righteous, or arrogant position. Nor is he suggesting that wisdom is reserved for a select few. Rather, he is speaking about the status of all the baptized who are called to enter into full knowledge of the Son of God. By renewing our minds, we cooperate with our baptismal grace that we might be counted among the spiritually mature.

The Seed of Virtue: Acting Upon God's Grace

In his series of books, *In Conversation with God,* Francis Fernandez writes,

> *The work of sanctification belongs entirely to God in his infinite goodness. Nevertheless, he has willed that correspondence on the part of human beings is necessary, and has consequently placed in our nature the capacity for disposing ourselves towards receiving the supernatural action of grace. Through cultivating human virtues—resilience, loyalty, truthfulness, affection, courtesy—we prepare our soul in the best possible way for the action of the Holy Spirit.*[7]

What Are the Virtues?

What are the virtues, and why are they necessary for our progress in the spiritual life and our quest for holiness? The *Catechism* defines virtue as "an habitual and firm disposition to do the good" (#1803).

In order for a good action to become a virtue, it must be practiced consistently and with resolution. This begins to establish an interior disposition—a "good habit," if you will. The more a virtue is practiced, the greater is the likelihood that it will become a part of us, a way of behavior which identifies our character and punctuates our daily life.

Virtuous living is not a concept that began with Christianity. In fact, the ancient moral philosophers recommended that only through adherence to the virtues could an individual attain his full human potential and achieve harmony in his life. Aristotle, in particular, identifies four virtues that relate to daily life and interaction with neighbor, which he called the "cardinal" virtues.

The Cardinal Virtues

The word "cardinal," in this context, is derived from the word "cardo" (hinge), because everything in the moral life, and all other virtues, hinge on these. The cardinal virtues are *fortitude, justice, prudence,* and *temperance.*

St. Thomas Aquinas taught that the moral virtues of the ancients become laden with supernatural power when infused with the grace of God. When this happens, not only do the virtues enable us to live worthy lives, but they become indispensable aids for us and for our neighbor as we journey toward salvation. Thus, through our cooperation with God's grace to live a virtuous life, our practice of the Christian virtues becomes a conduit of supernatural action in the world.

Fortitude is the virtue that gives us moral courage. It builds strength of resolve, and helps us to remain resolute in the face of difficulties and trials. Fortitude helps us to resist temptation and to stay strong in the face of persecution. When fortitude is practiced regularly, we live out our call to be a "soldier for Jesus Christ." Speaking the truth when it may cost us position or status, maintaining godly convictions in the face of disagreement, standing holy ground when confronted with injustice, deciding for truth in the midst of moral conflict—in all of these ways fortitude gives us strength.

Justice is practiced when we give to God what is God's, and to our neighbor what is our neighbor's. The *Catechism of the Catholic Church* tells us, "Justice toward men disposes one to respect the rights of each and to establish in human relationships the harmony that promotes equity with regard to persons and to the common good" (#1807).

Justice requires that we respect the rights of the individual, his good name, and all that he owns. Laws of the land must be just and fair, reflect the dignity and worth of the human person, and be equitable for all—the defenseless, the weak, the poor, the indigent, and the elderly. Justice requires that employers treat employees with loyalty, fairness, and honesty. In like fashion, the same disposition applies to the employee's attitude toward his employer and job. These are only a few of the ways in which social justice is demonstrated. Through the virtue of justice, interpersonal relationships reflect the face of a just and holy God.

Prudence disposes us toward right judgment in practical and spiritual matters. A prudent action follows three steps—deliberation, decision, and execution. First, we reflect about the decision and evaluate it according to the standards of God, seeking counsel if necessary. Next, we judge wisely—leaving aside personal preference, bias, and preconceived notions—and make our decision with resolve. Finally, we execute our decision without procrastination, without vacillation, and without doubt.[8]

Cultivating the virtue of prudence helps us maintain balance in our daily life as well as our spiritual life. As we read in the *Catechism*, "With the help of this virtue we apply moral principles to particular cases without error and overcome doubts about the good to achieve and the evil to avoid" (#1806).

Temperance, the final cardinal virtue, is the virtue of self-control. Without temperance, we would give in to the passions of the world and the passions of the flesh. Temperance calls us to moderate all sensual pleasures, and prevents us from slipping into sexual lust, gluttony, and all forms of addiction including drunkenness, gambling, and consumerism.

Temperance puts a shield of grace around the five senses and helps us order them to a worthy end. This virtue is greatly needed in our world today where overindulgence is encouraged, applauded, and extolled. Through the virtue of temperance, we can give good example and become beacons of light that encourage others to live a life of self-control.

From Flowers of Virtue, the Fruit of the Spirit

As we begin to practice the cardinal virtues of fortitude, justice, prudence, and temperance, other virtues begin to bloom. From fortitude comes patience, long-suffering, service to others; justice yields self-sacrifice, obedience, faithfulness to religious practice; prudence begets foresight, circumspection, fidelity; from temperance bud chastity, meekness, poverty of spirit, and mortification.

From the cardinal virtues the nourishing fruit of the Holy Spirit is born—love, joy, peace, patient endurance, kindness, generosity, faith, mildness, and self-control.

Remember, however, that though the cardinal virtues grow as a beautiful and nourishing tree in the garden of our heart, they do not come of themselves. Rather, the cardinal virtues are rooted deeply in the life of still other virtues. And these virtues find their source in God Himself. They are the theological virtues.

The Theological Virtues

The theological virtues are "theological" because they are a participation in the very life of God. The *Catechism* teaches that these virtues are infused into our souls through the Sacrament of Baptism, and "are the foundation of Christian moral activity; they animate it and give it its special character. They inform and give life to all the moral virtues. They are infused by God into the souls of the faithful to make them capable of acting as His children and of meriting eternal life. They are the pledge of the presence and action of the Holy Spirit in the faculties of the human being" (#1813). The theological virtues are faith, hope, and charity.

Faith enables us to believe in God and to accept His revelation as truth. Therefore, faith is the foundation of our spiritual life. Faith justifies us; faith sanctifies us; and faith unites us to God. Faith justifies us because it is the means God uses to bring us into relationship with Him. St. Paul tells us in Hebrews 11:6, "Whoever would draw near to God must believe that He exists, and that He rewards those who seek Him." God plants the seed of faith into our soul in Baptism so that throughout our lives it might continue to bring us ever closer to His Divine Life.

Faith also sanctifies us. In his book *The Spiritual Life*, Father Adolphe Tanquerey writes, "Faith is the root of sanctity.... Roots, if deep, lend solidity to the tree they sustain; so the soul, imbedded in faith, withstands spiritual storms. Hence, deep faith is of capital importance in order to attain a high degree of perfection."[9] Finally, faith unites us to God because it is a participation in the very life of the Trinity. Through faith, we see with the eyes of God.

Hope produces trust in God, just as faith enables us to believe in God. "Hope is the theological virtue by which we desire the kingdom of heaven and eternal life as our happiness, placing our trust in Christ's promises and relying not on our own strength, but on the help of the grace of the Holy Spirit" (*Catechism*, #1817).

While we hope for many answers to prayer in this life, our ultimate hope is that we spend all eternity in heaven with God. For this reason, we cultivate hope by meditating on the power of God and the promises of God with which Sacred Scripture is replete. In prayerfully reading about God's consistent faithfulness to His people, we grow in the hopeful expectation that we will see His faithfulness manifested in our lives, and that this faithfulness will bring our earthly sojourn to its ultimate destination of heaven. Hope in God is much different from the hope which springs from human desire or yearning, for we are hoping in the One who promises that He will bring to completion in us the good work He has begun.

Charity, the third theological virtue, is God's own love active within us. Because charity is a participation in the very life of God, it differs from human love. While human love is conditional, charity (God's love) is not. Jesus tells us that we must love God with our whole heart, with our whole soul, with our whole mind, and we must love our neighbor as ourselves. This commandment would be impossible to keep were it not for the virtue of charity.

Through the theological virtue of charity, God's own love takes up residence within us, thus enabling us to love *through His love* rather than our own. Through charity we love the unlovable, forgive the unforgivable, show mercy to the merciless. Through charity hearts are mended, spirits are restored, and souls are made whole. Only through charity can we, as women, fulfill our mission to be the healers of the world.

Living the Virtues

Where and when are we to practice virtue? We need not go far in our search for an answer, for every day provides us with ample opportunities. In fact, when we look at the events of our day in light of God's will of good pleasure, we recognize every situation as an opportunity for growth in holiness, calling forth a virtuous response from us in cooperation with God's grace. As we become attuned to the hand of God moving in and through all things, we no longer look at trials as obstacles to be overcome, but rather as blessings, laden with grace waiting to be discovered. Difficult circumstances become the olive press of sanctity from which flows the unction of God's love.

And, though we work within the confines of human ability and prayer to resolve each problem, we reap great spiritual benefit as we persevere through the trial until the answer comes. Virtue is not practiced in a vacuum, but within the context of our everyday lives.

God is calling us to holiness of life, and the virtues help us attain that goal. How, then, do we hone our spiritual sight to uncover the great gift hidden within the circumstance that occasions it? We do it through spiritual reflection—a contemplative look at God's action within us, around us, among us.

The Seed of Holy Reflection: Seeing the Hand of God in Daily Life

The gift of wisdom is a "contemplative" gift. If we desire to cultivate wisdom, then we must discern God's action in the circumstances and situations of our lives. This contemplation is not self-absorption nor a disordered introspection, but rather a holy contemplation through which we perceive God's will for us. The spiritual practice of evaluating our life's events through the eyes of faith will help us attain true wisdom and understanding, and will enable us to reap the spiritual benefits God offers us through each circumstance.

Our Mother in the order of grace, the Blessed Virgin Mary, provides us with a wonderful example of one who practiced this form of reflection. Twice in his Gospel, St. Luke states that the Blessed Virgin Mary *"pondered all these things in her heart."* What St. Luke is telling us in this description of our Mother is that she evaluated all of life's events in light of God's Word.

Recall that Mary was a faithful Jewish girl, raised in the religion of her people. She was a child of prayer who had developed an intimate relationship with Yahweh. The psalms and the words of the prophets were familiar to her, and she had made them the rumination of her heart.

Thus, she understood that God was speaking through Gabriel when the angel asked her to be the mother of the Messiah, even though Mary could not understand how this was physically possible. The angel's message echoed the words spoken by the prophets who heralded His coming. Her understanding of the ways of God and the promises He made through the prophets gave her the faith to trust and surrender at this all-important moment in her life.

This prayerful disposition of evaluating the events of life in light of the Word of God did not change for Mary our Mother when Jesus was born. In fact, her close union with the Son of God, *in utero* and after His birth, must have given her keener insight into the ways of God. A human creature, Mary was not omniscient. However, through her intimate union with God, she was infused with spiritual knowledge. From such holy wisdom, Mary interpreted all of her life's events—the birth of her Son, Simeon's prophecy, the flight into Egypt, the finding of the Child in the temple, the wedding feast at Cana, Jesus' teaching and healing ministry, His Passion, death, and resurrection, His ascension into heaven, the day of Pentecost—and invested into them her faith and trust in God's revelation *even as it was being revealed.*

Called to Ponder

Following after our Mother in the order of grace, we are called into a similar kind of prayerful contemplation. We must learn to measure all of life's events, all of the circumstances and situations of the world, against God's Word and revelation. If we are to evaluate with the mind of God, we, too, must *"ponder all these things in our hearts"* in our daily time of prayer.

As we practice this form of prayerful reflection, we will see the hand of God moving in all of the situations of our lives—through the joyful times and through the sorrowful times. Our knowledge of God will grow, our human vision and understanding will be infused with the Divine Life, and we will gain true wisdom, insight, and spiritual judgment. Thus, like our Mother, we will invest our faith and trust in God's revelation to us *even as it is being revealed,* and with complete abandon we will cast ourselves into God's arms of love.

A prayer-time reflection. I recall a prayer meditation from my own life that showed me the value of pondering the events of our lives through the eyes of God—even those times of trial. Matthew 2:1-12 describes the journey of the Magi to the Christ Child. As I reflected upon this passage, in my mind's eye I could see the Magi. They traversed the country, their pace set by the deliberate movement of the camels, their every step illuminated by a brilliant light streaming from the heavens.

In my imagination I could hear them talking excitedly about the marvelous star that rose in the East—a star that obviously signified the birth of a child who would alter world history. *This must be His star, the star of the Child whom the Jews expect to be their new King, their Messiah,* my imagination heard them say. I could hear these astrologers remarking about the marvelous star, and what a great privilege it was to have discovered it, to travel under its brilliant glow, and to follow it in order to give homage to this new king. *What an honor!* I could almost hear them say.

I followed them in my mind's eye as they continued their journey. I watched them look up to the sky in disappointment when the star disappeared, forcing them to stop in Jerusalem to consult the Jews as to the whereabouts of the baby king. Imagine their profound elation upon seeing the star when it reappeared, leading them directly to the place where the Christ Child was.

What awe must have filled them when they beheld the Son of God! How their senses must have been overcome by the sight of the Incarnate Word! Did their hearts thrill at His tender smile? Were their souls saturated with peace and joy and hope as they looked at Him? Could they have imagined such a wondrous encounter?

These questions flooded my mind as I allowed my imagination to freely follow the Magi to their ultimate destination. As I prayed, I contemplated this story's significance in my own life. Why had the Holy Spirit given me this reading at this time? Again and again my attention was drawn back to the star.

The glorious star was God's own compass, which directed the wise men of the Orient—Gentiles—to the Christ Child. Clearly, they were transformed by the experience, drawn into a life-changing encounter with God's only begotten Son. They risked their own lives to protect this Child, returning home by another route instead of reporting back to Herod, as the king had instructed.

As I continued to pray, I considered the "stars" in my own life: the people and circumstances God used to lead me to Jesus.

Certainly my parents, who raised me in a Catholic home, were recognizable "stars" in my journey to Christ. So, too, my Catholic education imparted to me by the Vincentian Sisters of Charity and the Dominican Sisters. Continued study of the faith shone as an illuminating force which drew me closer still to the heart of God.

My husband, who loves me so completely, and our children, the fruit of our marriage, have been radiant stars lighting my way. The Marian Servants of Divine Providence,[10] the Private Association of the Christian Faithful to which I belong, good and holy friends whose support and own love of God are lights themselves, were obvious stars, brilliant and lasting.

Still other stars quickly appeared. These stars were so glorious their golden rays all but blinded the eye. The sacraments glistened like diamonds in a velvet black sky. The Holy Sacrifice of the Mass shone with the brilliance of the noonday sun. Eucharist and Adoration of the Blessed Sacrament radiated with a splendor too effulgent to be viewed by the naked eye. And private prayer, that personal holy time of conversing with God, was a steady and faithful light illuminating the way to Jesus Christ.

Then I noticed other stars, too … stars that appeared murky and dull, their radiance shrouded by thick, dense fog. Dark clouds obscured their light, and the roadway below them was shadowed and veiled. *What were these "stars" in my life?* I wondered.

Almost immediately, the clouds broke and the fog dissipated to reveal the unique grandeur of these stars. These stars represented the difficult moments in my life—the trials and tribulations, the times of intense sorrow and pain, torment and disappointment, misunderstanding and hurt. These were the circumstances and events I always categorized as "purification" and "testing."

Now the Holy Spirit was showing me that these were moments of great blessing and light, moments filled with heavenly illumination. For these were the moments when I was most dependent upon God, seeking His guidance and direction. These were the moments when angels ministered to me and saints interceded for me. These were the moments when Jesus lovingly carried me from minute to minute in capable and loving arms. These were the moments when, though I felt bereft of His presence, I was closest to His Most Sacred Heart. Indeed, these were the moments when glorious streams from heaven above broke through the darkness of my consciousness with the light of God's love.

Suddenly, these stars appeared more brilliant than all the rest, for in these moments the fruitful light of every other "star" in my life lent its radiance to lead me more deeply into the Divine Life itself.

Throughout the course of life, all of us experience many "stars"—people, circumstances, events, and situations—that can lead us closer to Christ. Some of these glow with heavenly illumination. Others are covered by the dark veil of tribulation. Yet, in the midst of it all, Jesus is with us, calling us to Himself, waiting to lead us more deeply into the Trinitarian Life.

Like the Blessed Virgin Mary let us "ponder in our hearts" every circumstance, each situation, evaluating it in the light of God's love. Our holy reflection will pierce the darkness and the radiance of God's plan for us will stream through. We will see every event and occurance as a star whose brilliant light calls us to the Christ Child.

Let us ask God to give us vision to recognize our "stars," grace to accept them, and true praise and joy as we embrace them, knowing His divine purpose for us can never be thwarted if our only desire is His holy will.

Spiritual Direction: Nurturing the Divine Life Within Us

Spiritual progress does not proceed on a straight line. Rather, it moves along a circuitous route, with bends and turns in the road that seem to lead us alternately *away from,* then *closer to,* our ideal. We make strides, fall back, gain insight, move forward—and each time we find that we are a little ahead of where we were in the first place. The same lessons present themselves again and again—lessons in trust, hope, perseverance, faith—but at each visitation, we penetrate the mystery more deeply and conform to the will of God more nearly.[11]

Gradually, we come to see that with each forward move we are growing in wisdom, age, and grace. The virtues of faith, hope, and charity are developing within us. Our thoughts, our actions, and the dispositions of our hearts are infused with the life of God. And so, in time, we achieve spiritual maturity.

At all stages of spiritual progress, we remain people who are inherently sinful, broken, weak, and in need of healing. Thus, our intimations in prayer, our discernment on issues with others, and our relationship with God can be clouded or impaired. Sometimes we find that as we grow closer to God, we don't always know how to respond to Him; or we may sense that we have lost our way or gotten off the path to holiness. The quality of our prayer may change and new heights and valleys appear within the landscape of our soul. Doubts, scruples, confusion, or temptation may begin to plague our path. For all of these reasons, when we are serious about pursuing the spiritual life, we must have a spiritual director. Though spiritual direction is not necessary for sanctification, it is a normal way of making spiritual progress and growing in the gift of wisdom.

What Is Spiritual Direction?

At every stage of the spiritual life, those who are serious about a life of prayer and spiritual growth need the wise advice and counsel of another who can offer necessary guidance and direction along the way toward spiritual perfection. Thomas Dubay, in his book *Seeking Spiritual Direction: How to Grow the Divine Life Within,* defines spiritual direction as "the guiding of a person into a life truly under the dominion of the Holy Spirit, who is the primary director."[12]

Both the purpose and benefits of spiritual direction are distinct from other Christian practices and disciplines. It is not the same as "holy conversation" with others or the directives and corrections offered by the priest in the confessional. Spiritual direction is not psychotherapy; nor does it follow popular and cultural trends like Eastern Oriental mysticism or personality typing. Rather, it is a consistent and systematic program established by the director to lead a soul to Christian perfection.

The History of Spiritual Direction

Spiritual direction has long been practiced in the Church as a means of helping souls grow in spiritual understanding and holy wisdom. Perhaps the first instance of it in the early Church takes place with St. Paul on the road to Damascus. Though our Lord Himself appeared to Paul at the moment of the apostle's conversion, He then sent him to Ananias for instruction (see Acts 9:3-9).

In reference to the conversion of Paul, Pope Leo XIII says,

> *God, in His infinite Providence, has decreed that men for the most part should be saved by men; hence He has appointed that those whom He calls to a loftier degree of holiness should be led thereto by*

men, "in order that," as Chrysostom says, "we should be taught by God through men...." Those who reject [this doctrine], assuredly do so rashly and at their peril.[13]

The last two sentences in this quote by Pope Leo XIII refer to the advice the great saints give on the matter of spiritual direction. St. Francis de Sales advises, "Do you seriously wish to travel the road to devotion? If so, look for a good man to guide and lead you. This is the most important of all words of advice."[14] Similarly, St. John of the Cross says, "The soul that is alone and without a master, and has virtue, is like the burning coal that is alone. It will grow colder rather than hotter."[15]

Another saint of the spiritual life, St. John Climacus, tells us, "In the same way that a ship with a good pilot arrives safely in port, so also, will the soul that has a good shepherd safely reach its destination even though it may many times have gone astray."[16] And St. Teresa of Avila advises her sisters, "However many consolations and pledges of love the Lord may give you ... you must never be so sure of yourselves that you cease to be afraid of falling back again, and you must keep yourselves from occasions of sin. Do all you can to discuss these graces and favours with someone who can give you light and have no secrets from him."[17]

Spiritual direction helps us make progress in Christian perfection in a number of ways. Dubay outlines these as the most apparent benefits:

Spiritual Direction helps us to:
- *Detect mediocrity or inner weakness*
- *Handle periods of difficult, dry prayer*
- *Do appropriate penance*
- *Carefully moderate enthusiasm for extraordinary phenomena*
- *Discern a vocation*

- *Exercise wisdom in reading material*
- *Detect shadings among virtues and vices*
- *Identify psychological problems*
- *Assess spiritual progress or the lack of it*
- *Acquire accountability and experience support.*[18]

In his classic work, *The Three Ages of the Interior Life*, Reginald Garrigou-Lagrange sums it up well:

> *Everyone knows that a guide is needed in order to climb a mountain without difficulty. The same thing happens when it is a matter of a spiritual climb ... and even more so in that here one must avoid the pitfalls set by the devil, who dearly wants to bring us down.*[19]

With all of these benefits, the next question is: Who makes a good spiritual director?

Qualities to Seek in a Spiritual Director

St. Francis de Sales sums up the necessary qualities of a spiritual director in three words—charity, knowledge, and prudence. "If he lacks one of these," says St. Francis, "there is danger."[20] St. Teresa of Avila agrees. In her autobiography she writes,

> *It is of great consequence that the director should be prudent—I mean, of sound understanding—and a man of experience. If, in addition to this, he is a learned man, it is a very great matter. But if these three qualities cannot be had together, the first two are the most important, because learned men may be found with whom we can communicate when it is necessary. I mean, that for beginners learned men are of little use, if they are not men of prayer. I do not say that they are to have nothing to do with learned men.... Learning is a great thing.... From silly devotions, God deliver us!*[21]

Today, "silly devotions" abound. All kinds of fads and superficial exercises are passed off as spiritual direction or methods useful in the spiritual life. It takes a learned, prudent, and loving director to lead us through the minefields of spiritual nonsense that clutter many retreat houses, universities, and parishes today. Like St. Francis and St. Teresa, St. John of the Cross recommends that a spiritual director possess learning, experience, and discretion.[22] With these three characteristics, a directee can feel comfortable that wise advice and good counsel will be given.

Thomas Dubay recommends one additional qualification of a worthy spiritual director in *Seeking Spiritual Direction.* He suggests: "There must be neither naive credulity nor closeminded skepticism when one hears of unusual happenings narrated by the directee. We have in mind especially divine enlightenments of sundry types … and absorbing and ecstatic prayer."[23]

Skilled spiritual directors know how to recognize authentic spiritual experiences, and can lead us away from deceptions and illusions that can distract us—or even seduce us away from truth.

Spiritual Directors: Choose Wisely
Since charity, knowledge, and prudence are the qualities we seek in a spiritual director, we must be careful not to choose someone who lacks these qualities.

Is he or she knowledgeable? If the director does not adhere to gospel standards or approaches them with a "relativistic" bent, or if the director does not promote the teaching of the Roman Catholic Church, he or she is immediately unsuitable.

In addition, the spiritual director should be theologically trained or certified in spiritual direction through an institution known for quality of education and orthodoxy. The spiritual director must also have experience both in direction and in personal prayer. The nuances of the spiritual life are many, and only one practiced in discerning the movements of the soul can adequately guide us.

Is he or she prudent? How do we know if a spiritual director lacks prudence? This can be seen in the quality of direction we are given.

If the spiritual director's main concern is with something other than conforming our will to the divine will, we should be wary.

If the director's view of God is anything other than theistic (only one God), we should be wary.

If we are urged to participate in oriental techniques of prayer such as Zen, transcendental meditation, or yoga, we should be wary.

If the director advises us to gain self-knowledge through the enneagram, personality typing, or Jungian psychology, we should be wary. If he or she suggests any New Age or occult techniques, we should be wary.

Finally, if the spiritual director rushes to judgment, makes quick evaluations, suggests easy answers, or makes light of our concerns and questions, we should be wary. All of these are good indications that the person may lack prudence and sound judgment.

Is he or she charitable? How do we know if a spiritual director acts out of charity? The way he treats us is the first indicator. Does the spiritual director treat us as an individual or does he try to "plug" our responses into a preconceived mold? Dubay says,

> *God has countless ways of dealing with each soul. Some directors make the mistake of leaving aside most norms and patterns in an exaggerated flexibility, while others apply principles as if there were no individual differences in the capacity and development of their disciples.*[24]

There are other ways that we can judge if our spiritual director exercises charity. Is he or she interested in what we have to say? How are his or her listening skills? Is he or she compassionate and sympathetic?

However, a word of caution must be issued here. While our spiritual director must exercise true charity, it is not his or her job to agree with us, be easy on us, or make concessions for us. The job of a spiritual director is to lead us in the way of sanctity and Christian perfection. The spiritual life is not an easy road. It is narrow and it is rigorous. We must expect the truth to be spoken to us, but we can expect it to be spoken in love.

What Should Be My Attitude Toward My Spiritual Director?

While there are expectations we must have for our spiritual director, there are also expectations we must have of ourselves if we hope to make full use of the direction process. In his book, *The Spiritual Life*, Father Adolphe Tanquerey gives us clear guidance.[25]

First, we must respect our director as we would an ambassador of Christ, for that is who he or she is. Therefore, we must refrain from both undue criticism and untempered affection. St. Francis de Sales tells us that "In a word, this friendship should be strong and sweet, holy, all sacred, wholly divine and entirely spiritual."[26]

Second, we must approach our relationship with trust and openness of heart, willing to disclose to our director the interior movements of our heart, our thoughts and ideas, intimations we receive through prayer, and weaknesses and frailties we recognize. St. Francis says, "Open your heart to him with all sincerity and fidelity, tell him clearly and without deception or dissimulation about what is good in you and what is bad. By such means the good will be examined and approved and what is bad will be corrected and repaired.... You must have unlimited confidence in him, mingled with holy reverence, so that reverence will neither lessen confidence nor confidence hinder reverence."[27]

Third, we must be docile. Our hearts must be teachable and we must be willing to learn. Docility is practiced through faithfully carrying out our spiritual director's instructions, taking to heart his or her words of guidance, and following through on any suggestions we may receive. If we come to spiritual direction with hardness of heart exercised through a strong self-will, we can be certain to make little progress. But if we come to our time of direction truly seeking the face of the Lord and with docility of spirit, we will find ourselves growing strong in the spiritual life.

What if we discover that we have irreconcilable differences with our spiritual director, even though he or she may fulfill all of the necessary qualifications? Human nature is human nature. Sometimes, personalities are not well suited to each other. In these cases, we must explore all possible avenues to resolve these differences. Often, the cause of irritation is the very area in which we need healing, repentance, growth, virtue. As Tanquerey says, "Only a grave reason and mature reflection should determine us to seek another spiritual guide."[28]

What then would be legitimate reasons for changing a spiritual director? Tanquerey gives the following reasons: (1) Despite our best efforts, we cannot be open with our director because we do not respect or trust him or her. (2) We have reasonable fears that our director cannot lead us in holiness because of his or her beliefs, dispositions, or sentiments toward us. (3) We discover our director lacks charity, knowledge, or prudence. These are legitimate reasons to seek another director.[29] Remember, however, that consistency in the spiritual life is important; the benefit of continuity in spiritual direction cannot be overestimated.

What If I Can't Find a Spiritual Director?

This question is an important one, because in every age there seems to be a shortage of holy men and holy women who can lead others on the road to holiness and help them nurture the Divine

Life within. Saints Francis de Sales, Teresa of Avila, and John of the Cross all lamented the shortage of accomplished spiritual directors in their day; the Catholic lay faithful complain about it in ours. What, then, are we to do when we have made every attempt to find a spiritual director but no one is available or those who are available seem to be questionable?

Dubay offers several possible solutions, cautioning the reader against settling too quickly for these options without due effort to find a suitable director.[30]

First, make use of the Sacrament of Reconciliation. Though the main purpose of the sacrament is the absolving of sin and healing the wounds of the soul, the sacrament does provide an opportunity to seek advice. Dubay recommends that we select one question and phrase it succinctly. In most cases, the confessor will be only too happy to aid us in our spiritual walk.

Second, love truth and seek after it passionately. While many of us believe we are earnest in our search for truth, the fact is that we often are looking only for agreement and complicity. We must seek to conform our mind with reality, not with fad or pleasure or self-will. "Seek, and you will find," Jesus tells us (Mt 7:7). If we search for truth, we will find it, for God gives us the desires of our heart (see Ps 37:4).

Third, pursue holiness. We discussed how to grow in holiness earlier in this book. Prayer is absolutely essential, as is the desire to rid ourselves of vices, attachments, and any other hindrances to union with God. We must also practice obedience to God's will. Without obedience, we will never even begin the spiritual life, much less grow in holiness.

Fourth, we must accept the circumstances of our lives and embrace God's will of good pleasure. It is through the cross of Christ that we attain the light we need for the spiritual life. And it is through the Passion lived out in our own lives that we are able to experience the resurrection, power, and joy that come through uniting ourselves to the suffering of Christ. As Dubay says, "We can be sure of doing the divine will both in striving to stem the tide of what is wrong and in suffering well what cannot be prevented."[31]

Fifth, we must pray. Prayer is the dynamic of relationship that leads us into union with God. Through our time of prayer, we grow in wisdom, age, and grace before the Lord as His very life is poured into the humble confines of our hearts. We discover His love for us, and through this recognition, we can trust, surrender, and receive all that He desires for us.

Finally, we can seek spiritual guidance through holy reading and by studying the lives of the saints. Much that passes today for "spiritual literature" can lead us along the path of perdition rather than the road of holiness. For this reason, we must be discriminating in what we select. It is best to stay with publishers who are known for their orthodoxy. Even then, we must be circumspect, weeding from our shelves anything that seems to make a formula of the spiritual life or to trivialize the truths of our Faith.

We must exercise wisdom in which books we choose. "By their fruits you shall know them," we are told; this is a good way to assess the worth of authors. If there is any question, it is best to avoid them. The classics and writings of the saints are safe reading material and can do much to lead us in sanctity. So, too, with Sacred Scripture, the *Catechism of the Catholic Church,* and standard works such as the writings of the Church Fathers. A work of which I am particularly fond is *In Conversation with God,* by

Francis Fernandez. This seven-volume set uses the daily readings of the liturgy to provide us with spiritual food that nourishes our minds, feeds our souls, and satisfies our hearts. Indeed, it is spiritual direction for daily living.

By reading and studying the lives of the saints, we come to know those luminaries of the Faith whose own path to holiness has lit the way for countless numbers of souls. Teresa of Avila, John of the Cross, Francis de Sales, Ignatius of Loyola, Thérèse of Lisieux, and Catherine of Siena are just a small number of those saints who have become beacons of light in the spiritual life. Learning how they prayed, how they handled suffering, and how they united their wills to God provides us with clear guidance and certain direction.

Dubay tells us that "divine reading" consists of three elements which make it different from other forms of reading: (1) "it nourishes a person with God's word, even when the content is not expressly biblical"; (2) "it enlightens the reader with divine truth"; and (3) "it is a prayer experience, a dialogue with the indwelling Lord living within his Church and in each member in his temple."[32] Certainly, the writings of the saints and the lives of the saints accomplish all three purposes.

A Closing Word on Wisdom

Pope John Paul II gives us wise counsel on growth in the spiritual life. He tells us, *"To be able to discover the actual will of the Lord in our lives always involves the following: a receptive listening to the Word of God and the Church, fervent and constant prayer, recourse to a wise and loving spiritual guide, and a faithful discernment of the gifts and talents given by God, as well as the diverse social and historic situations in which one lives."* [33]

If we are going to fulfill our call as women who *"aid humanity in not falling"* and are the healers of the world, it is essential that we cultivate the fruit of wisdom in our lives. Longing to live out the fullness of our mission, we must approach each day with the mind of Christ. Conforming to the will of God, renewing the mind through obedience, practicing the virtues, contemplative reflection, spiritual direction, and docility to the movement of the Holy Spirit—in all these ways we grow in wisdom and make progress in the spiritual life.

As we come to the close of our chapter on wisdom, we would do well to consider the following words from Sirach. They provide us with a succinct review of this chapter and give us clear guidance on attaining wisdom, "the spiritual vision" of the abundant life:

If you wish, you can be taught;
> *if you apply yourself, you will be shrewd.*
If you are willing to listen, you will learn;
> *if you give heed, you will be wise.*
Frequent the company of the elders;
> *whoever is wise, stay close to him.*
Be eager to hear every godly discourse;
> *let no wise saying escape you.*
If you see a man of prudence, seek him out;
> *let your feet wear away his doorstep!*
Reflect on the precepts of the Lord,
> *let his commandments be your constant meditation;*
Then he will enlighten your mind,
> *and the wisdom you desire he will grant.*

SIRACH 6:32-37, NAB

SIX

Eucharist: Heart of the Abundant Life

*L*ike Mary, our Mother, we have been called by God to bring the life of Jesus Christ to the world. And like our Mother, we, too, must be impregnated by the spirit of the gospel, imbued by the One whose name is Jesus Christ. We have considered the supreme degree to which our Holy Mother, assimilated to the Word of God, became a reflection of Him whom she bore. She models for us the degree of transformation to which each of us is called.

Prayer, obedience, and acting with the wisdom of God lead us on the path of transformation. But it is when we receive into our bodies the One whose image we wish to reflect that we are most powerfully transformed. As Mary conceived Jesus in the confines of her body, we, too, are to conceive Him in the wombs of our hearts. Through the gift of the Eucharist, we receive the very person of Jesus Christ, and in so doing become a chalice of His life.

Come, Let Us Adore Him

To the extent we receive the Eucharist with faith and conviction and adore the Heart of our Lord as given to us in the Blessed Sacrament, we encourage the transformation process God has begun in us. Pope Paul VI tells us that "anyone who approaches this august sacrament with special devotion ... experiences how great is the value of communing with Christ ... for there is nothing more effective for advancing on the road to holiness."[1]

Recent polls suggest that less than half of Catholics in the United States who attend Mass believe in the Real Presence of Jesus in the Eucharist. These are not "C & E" Catholics, the Christmas and Easter variety. Nor do they belong to the group who step inside the church only to be "hatched, matched, and dispatched." Rather, they are teachers in our Catholic schools, directors of religious education in our parishes, deacons, religious sisters, CCD instructors, mothers, fathers, grandparents, and yes, even parish priests! Basically, they form a random sampling of the entire Catholic population in America. What a pity! At every moment of the day throughout the world, Jesus offers Himself to us in the form of bread and wine so that we might be nourished with His own Body and Blood. And we, suffering from spiritual blindness, do not recognize Him in the breaking of the bread.

Sad as this fact is, however, we should not be surprised. St. Paul says to the Romans, "And how can they believe in him of whom they have not heard? And how can they hear without someone to preach?... Thus faith comes from what is heard" (Rom 10:14, 17, NAB). For decades now, many people have not heard the Good News that Jesus is fully present—body and blood, soul and divinity—in the consecrated host.

Authentic catechesis on the Real Presence has been absent from many religion classes for many years. This omission spans catechetical instruction from elementary schools to seminary courses. Many people under the age of forty have never been to any form of Eucharistic adoration. However, they are not to be blamed. They only need to be instructed so that the spiritual benefits of the Eucharist can become a transforming agent in their lives.

I Am the Bread of Life

If we are to reap the fullness of grace that the Eucharist offers us, then we must first *believe* that we are receiving the Body and Blood of our Lord Jesus Christ. To fortify our own belief, or to help those who do not believe, we should know what Jesus Himself tells us about the gift He offers.

Reading the sixth chapter of the Gospel of John (vv. 25-71), we discover that the crisis of faith surrounding the Real Presence is not new. In fact, it caused the first division in the body of Christ. Here Jesus referred to Himself as the *Bread of Life:* "I am the living bread which came down from heaven; if any one eats of this bread, he will live for ever; and the bread which I shall give for the life of the world is my flesh" (Jn 6:51). Finding this a hard teaching, the disciples murmured among themselves, asking one another, "How can he give us his flesh to eat?"

At these words the Jews grew angry, and their murmurs broke into quarreling. Jesus responded, "Truly, truly, I say to you, unless you eat the flesh of the Son of man and drink his blood, you have no life in you.... For my flesh is food indeed, and my blood is drink indeed. He who eats my flesh and drinks my blood abides in me, and I in him" (Jn 6:53, 55-56). So that there could not be any doubt as to what He meant, Jesus emphasized this statement by saying, "Truly, truly, I say to you," over and over again (Jn 6:26, 32, 47, 53).

The disciples' confusion gave way to outrage. "This is a hard saying; who can listen to it?" they complained (Jn 6:60). "How can anyone take it seriously?" No doubt they envisioned a cannibalistic ritual. Knowing this, Jesus wanted to put their minds at ease, so He prophesied about His own ascension and alluded to the Last Supper where He would change bread and wine into His own Body and Blood.

"Do you take offense at this?" He asked them. "Then what if you were to see the Son of man ascending where he was before? It is the spirit that gives life; the flesh is of no avail; the words I have spoken to you are spirit and life. But there are some of you that do not believe" (Jn 6:61-64). His body would *ascend to where it was before,* Jesus assured His followers, and they would witness this event. However, *through the power of the Holy Spirit who gives life,* He would give His flesh and blood in a supernatural and mysterious way.

Even with this explanation, Jesus knew many would not believe Him. He also knew one of those nonbelievers would betray Him. Scripture says, "Jesus knew from the first who those were that did not believe, and who it was that should betray Him. And he said, 'This is why I have told you that no one can come to me unless it is granted him by the Father'" (Jn 6:64-65). And, immediately after He spoke these words, many of Jesus' disciples did indeed leave Him. Scripture says, "After this many of his disciples drew back and no longer went about with him" (Jn 6:66). Thus, it is the discourse on the Body and Blood that caused the first schism, the first protest, the first rebellion among the followers of Christ. Each time we deny the central reality of the Eucharist—that it is indeed the Body and Blood, soul and divinity of Jesus Christ the Lord—we, like the doubting disciples, refuse the Messiah who is in our midst. Like them, we deny the truth and power of the One who is before us.

The belief that Jesus Christ is truly and substantially present in the Eucharist is a sign of true discipleship. In the closing verses of John 6, Peter demonstrated this mark of the true disciple when he responded to Jesus' question. As the unbelieving disciples walked away, Jesus turned to the Twelve and asked, "Will you also go away?" Simon Peter responded, "Lord, to whom shall we go? You have the words of eternal life; and we have believed, and have come to know, that you are the Holy One of God" (Jn 6:67-69).

May we, like Peter, be true disciples who acknowledge Jesus Christ, truly present in the Eucharist, and may we, like Peter, express our confidence in Him to others.

The Early Church Believed in the Real Presence

Belief in the Real Presence of Jesus in the Eucharist was universally held and taught by the early Church. Approximately A.D. 50, just seventeen years after the death, resurrection, and ascension of Jesus, St. Paul wrote to the Church at Corinth:

> *For I received from the Lord what I also delivered to you, that the Lord Jesus on the night when he was betrayed took bread, and when he had given thanks, he broke it, and said, "This is my body which is for you. Do this in remembrance of me." In the same way also the cup, after supper, saying, "This cup is the new covenant in my blood. Do this, as often as you drink it, in remembrance of me." For as often as you eat this bread and drink the cup, you proclaim the Lord's death until he comes. Whoever, therefore, eats the bread or drinks the cup of the Lord in an unworthy manner will be guilty of profaning the body and blood of the Lord. Let a man examine himself, and so eat of the bread and drink of the cup. For any one who eats and drinks without discerning the body eats and drinks judgment upon himself. That is why many of you are weak and ill, and some have died.*

1 CORINTHIANS 11:23-30

Here Paul tells the Corinthians that Jesus Himself instituted the Eucharist. Then he tells them that if a person receives the Body and Blood unworthily, he sins against the Body and Blood. Therefore, a person should examine himself to make certain he is not in a state of serious sin, *and also to make certain that he believes in the Eucharistic Presence.* If a person eats and drinks without recognizing Jesus, Paul says he drinks a judgment against himself. This judgment causes illness, infirmity, and death.

There is further evidence of the early Church's understanding of the Eucharistic Presence. St. Ignatius of Antioch wrote to the Smyrnaeans around A.D. 110 about those who held heterodox opinions. He wrote, "They abstain from the Eucharist and from prayer, because they do not confess that the Eucharist is the flesh of our Savior Jesus Christ, flesh which suffered for our sins and which the Father, in his goodness, raised up again."[2]

Writing just forty years after St. Ignatius, St. Justin Martyr wrote,

> *We call this food Eucharist, and no one else is permitted to partake of it, except one who believes our teaching to be true.... For not as common bread or common drink do we receive these; but since Jesus Christ our Savior was made incarnate by the Word of God and had both flesh and blood for our salvation, so too, we have been taught, the food which has been made into the Eucharist by the Eucharistic prayer set down by him ... is both the flesh and the blood of that incarnated Jesus.*[3]

Toward the end of the second century, St. Irenaeus of Lyons wrote this in his work *Against Heresies,* "[Christ] has declared the cup, a part of creation, to be his own Blood ... and the bread, a part of creation, he has established to be his own Body."[4] In 373, St. Athanasius, Bishop of Alexandria, said, "But after the great and wonderful prayers have been completed, then the bread is become the Body, and the wine the Blood, of our Lord Jesus Christ."[5] And, in the middle of the fourth century, St. Cyril of Jerusalem told the listeners of his sermon, "Do not, therefore, regard the Bread and Wine as simply that; for they are, according to the Master's declaration, the Body and Blood of Christ ... let your faith make you firm."[6] Further, in the fifth century, St. Augustine, doctor of the Church, wrote copiously about the Real Presence of Jesus in the Eucharist. In his *Sermons* he wrote, "You ought to know what you have received, what you are going to receive, and what you ought to receive daily. That Bread which you see on the altar, having been sanctified by the Word of God, is the Body of Christ. The chalice, or rather, what is in that chalice, having been sanctified by the Word of God, is the Blood of Christ."[7] And, in the thirteenth century, St. Thomas Aquinas wrote that by divine power, "the whole substance of the bread is changed into the whole substance of Christ's body, and the whole substance of the wine into the whole substance of Christ's blood."[8]

From the beginning, Magisterium teaching has always been firm on the Real Presence. The doctrine of transubstantiation was formally defined at the Fourth Lateran Council, and it was reiterated at the Council of Trent in 1551. The Council Fathers state "that after the consecration of bread and wine, our Lord Jesus Christ, true God and true man, is truly, really and substantially contained in the august sacrament of the Holy Eucharist under the appearance of those sensible things" and that in the Most Blessed Sacrament of the Eucharist, "the body and blood, together with the soul and divinity, of our Lord Jesus Christ, and, therefore, the whole Christ is truly, really, and substantially contained."[9]

Pope Paul VI wrote in *Mysterium Fidei* that by transubstantiation the bread and wine *are no longer common bread and common drink…. For beneath these appearances there is no longer what was there before but something quite different … since on the conversion of the bread and wine's substance, or nature, into the Body and Blood of Christ, nothing is left of the bread and wine but the appearances alone. Beneath these appearances Christ is present whole and entire, bodily present too, in his physical "reality," although not in the manner in which bodies are present in a place.*[10]

And, the *Catechism of the Catholic Church* states, "It is by the conversion of the bread and wine into Christ's body and blood that Christ becomes present in the sacrament…. The Eucharistic presence of Christ begins at the moment of the consecration and endures as long as the Eucharistic species subsists" (#1375, 1377). Belief in the Real Presence of Jesus in the Eucharist has always been a part of Church teaching and comes directly from the words of Jesus Christ. The preceding quotations are only a handful taken from the vast deposit of teaching on the Real Presence that is part of our Church history.

At every moment of every day, somewhere in the world, bread and wine become the Body and Blood of Jesus. Every day, we have the awesome opportunity to witness this holy act. And, if we are a Catholic in the state of grace, we can receive Jesus' own Body and Blood into the humble confines of our own being. On Holy Thursday, we commemorate the Last Supper, the historic moment when Jesus instituted this Most Blessed Sacrament. In St. Matthew's Gospel, we read:

Now as they were eating, Jesus took bread, and blessed and broke it, and gave it to the disciples and said, "Take, eat; this is my body." And he took a cup, and when he had given thanks, he gave it to them, saying, "Drink of it, all of you; for this is my blood of the new covenant, which is poured out for many for the forgiveness of sins."

MATTHEW 26:26-28

Through the gift of His Body and Blood, our Lord wants to transform us. He wants to heal us of our infirmities, nourish our souls, and fill us with purity and grace. Since the moment of the Last Supper to the present day this has always been the case. We have only to believe.

The Eucharistic Miracle of Lanciano

Church history is studded with many miracles of the Eucharist. These supernatural interventions of God are moments of grace ordained by the Father to increase our faith in His Son's Eucharistic Presence. Perhaps one of the most dramatic of these miracles is one which took place in Lanciano, Italy, a town whose history is interwoven with the crucifixion of Jesus.

In John's Gospel, we read,

The soldiers therefore came; and they broke the legs of the first, and of the other that was crucified with him. But after they were come to Jesus, when they saw that he was already dead, they did not break his legs. But one of the soldiers with a spear opened his side, and immediately there came out blood and water. And he that saw it, hath given testimony; and his testimony is true; that you also may believe. For these things were done, that the scripture might be fulfilled: "You shall not break a bone of him." And again another scripture saith: "They shall look on him whom they pierced."

JOHN 19:32-37 (Douay-Rheims)

Who was the soldier that pierced the side of Jesus, and what became of him? Tradition has it that his name was Longinus, a centurion who was born in a Roman town called Anxanum. In A.D. 33, sometime after being sent to Jerusalem, Longinus was ordered to preside at the crucifixion of Jesus. Upon thrusting his lance into the heart of our Lord, Longinus and his men were terror-stricken. Scripture recounts the awesome manifestations of God's power following the death of His Son, Jesus Christ: "The curtain of the temple was torn in two, from top to bottom; and the earth shook, and the rocks were split; the tombs also were opened, and many bodies of the saints who had fallen asleep were raised" (Mt 27:51-52).

Observing all that was happening, Longinus rightly proclaimed, "Truly this was the Son of God" (Mt 27:54). Tradition tells us that Longinus, who suffered from poor eyesight, dipped his fingers into the blood and water still trickling from the wounded heart of Jesus. As he touched his eyes with the blood and water, his eyesight was restored and his heart was converted. Longinus gave up his position in the Roman army, went to Cappadocia, and was eventually martyred for the faith. Some years later, his hometown, Anxanum, changed its name to Lanciano, *"The Lance,"* in honor of the saint who pierced the side of Jesus.

Perhaps it should be no surprise, then, that many years later the town of Lanciano, Italy, should be the location of another miracle involving the Precious Body and Blood. Like the story of Longinus, this story is also one of healing and conversion. In A.D. 700 a Basilian monk was faced with a crisis in his vocation. He did not believe in the Real Presence of Jesus in the Eucharist. Day after day, though he celebrated Mass according to the sacred tradition, a profound doubt in the Eucharistic Presence grew within him. Eventually, the moment of Consecration became a severe trial and a heartbreaking struggle. As he elevated the host and said the sacred words, guilt plagued his spirit and unrest tortured his soul. He prayed fervently to be released from this agony of doubt so that his vocation might be preserved.

On a particular morning during the celebration of the Mass, the monk was fighting an unusually strong attack of doubt. As the moment of Consecration approached, he earnestly beseeched God to relieve him of this terrible spiritual affliction. Then, he prayed the prayers of Consecration and elevated the host. Suddenly, he was transfixed by what he saw. His hands began to tremble. Soon, his whole body quaked in response to the miracle he was witnessing. Slowly, he turned and faced the congregation. As he did so, he spoke these words:

> *O fortunate witnesses to whom the Blessed God, to confound my disbelief, has wished to reveal Himself in this Most Blessed Sacrament and to render Himself visible to our eyes. Come, brethren, and marvel at our God so close to us. Behold the Flesh and Blood of our most beloved Christ.*

With these words, cries and wails filled the church. Shouts for mercy, pleas for forgiveness, tears of supplication ascended to the heavens in a symphony of worship and praise. For, as the congregation gazed upon the host in the hands of the Basilian monk, the people saw that it had become real flesh, and the wine real blood.

It would have been enough had this been the end of the miracle. Had the flesh and the blood eventually disintegrated, the miraculous revelation of the Real Presence of Jesus in the Eucharist would have been diminished in no way. However, without the use of any preservatives, defying the physical laws of nature, they remain to this day in the exact state as was first witnessed over twelve hundred years ago. Through the course of these twelve centuries many tests have been conducted on the transformed host and the contents of the chalice. The most recent testing was done in 1970. The scientific team used the most modern equipment available at the time. The team released the following six statements of their findings:

- *The flesh is real flesh. The blood is real blood.*

- *The flesh consists of the muscular tissue of the heart (myocardium).*

- *The flesh and blood belong to the human species.*

- *In the blood are proteins in the same normal proportions as found in the makeup of fresh, normal blood.*

- *The blood and the flesh were of the same blood type, AB; and the blood contains these minerals: chlorides, phosphorous, magnesium, potassium, sodium, and calcium.*

- *The preservation of the flesh and blood, which were left in their natural state for twelve centuries and exposed to the action of atmospheric and biological agents, remains an extraordinary phenomenon.*[11]

This marvelous ongoing miracle aids our faith in the Real Presence of Jesus today, just as it aided the faith of the people of God over twelve hundred years ago. It is only one of the many miracles throughout Church history that show us Jesus is truly present—Body and Blood, soul and divinity—in the Holy Eucharist.

And yet, this miracle appears to indicate something else to us as well. Through it, Jesus seems to be telling us that what He gives us in Holy Eucharist is His heart, the deepest part of His being, His innermost Self. We have only to ponder the transformative effect His Eucharistic Heart can have when we receive It with faith, hope, love, and conviction.

Preparing to Receive Jesus in the Eucharist

Through the Eucharist, Jesus desires to transform us into His image and likeness. The disposition with which we receive the Sacrament affects the spiritual benefit it renders in our lives.[12]

St. Catherine of Siena illustrates the effects of a fervent communion by this comparison:

> *If you had a burning lamp and all the whole world came to you for a light, the light of your lamp would not be diminished by the sharing, yet each person who shared it would have the whole light. True, each one's light would be more or less intense depending on what sort of material each brought to receive the fire. I give you this example so that you may better understand me. Imagine that many people brought candles, and one person's candle weighed one ounce, another's two or six, someone else's a pound, and yet another's more than that, and they all came to your lamp to light their candles. Each candle, the smallest as well as the largest, would have the whole light with all its heat and color and brightness. Still, you would think that the person who carried the one-ounce candle would have less than the one whose candle weighed a pound. Well, this is how it goes with those who receive this sacrament. Each one of you brings your own candle, that is, the holy desire with which you receive and eat this sacrament.[13]*

Jesus offers the totality of Himself to each one of us through the Blessed Eucharist. But the disposition or holy desire we bring to the Sacrament determines the degree of benefit we receive. If our disposition is weak and our fervency shallow, though we receive all of Jesus, the effect on our spirit is limited. However, if we come to the Sacrament with holy desire, we experience the full measure of grace Jesus offers to us through the gift of His Body and Blood.

In *The Three Ages of the Interior Life,* Father Reginald Garrigou-Lagrange identifies a fervent communion as one which is marked by humility, a profound respect for the Eucharist, a living faith, and an ardent desire to receive Jesus.[14] How, then, can we cultivate these dispositions of heart?

Humility

First, we must consciously remember who it is we are about to receive. Jesus—the only begotten Son of God, the Second Person of the Blessed Trinity, the Savior of the world—makes Himself available to you and to me. He is the Word Made Flesh, the Creator of the Universe, the Risen Messiah. Hidden in the humble appearance of bread and wine, He desires to enter into the confines of our body to be one with us. Do we deserve such a gift? No. But out of love, He comes to us nonetheless. We cultivate humility by acknowledging *who Jesus Christ is,* and who we are.

In addition to calling to mind the Person of Jesus Christ, we come to the Sacrament with humility when we prepare ourselves to receive the One who offers Himself to us. We prepare ourselves through interior recollection—a quiet time of prayer spent before Mass to still our thoughts as we come into the presence of Jesus Christ. Just as truly as Jesus was present at the Last Supper, so too is He present now. Just as truly as He changed bread and wine into His own Body and Blood in the Upper Room, so too will He do so now. We must strive to bring ourselves, with the help of God's grace, into the grace of the present moment.

Realizing that my finite mind could never penetrate this awesome mystery, I have a prayer that I say before Mass and again just prior to the Consecration. I pray, *"Dear Jesus, lead me more deeply into the Sacred Mystery that we are about to celebrate. Lead me more deeply into Your Eucharistic Presence."* This short little prayer, prayed with true desire, has had an immeasurable impact on my love of the Eucharist and its effect in my life.

Respect for the Eucharist

In the decades following the close of Vatican II, an attitude has swept through liturgical celebrations that is almost too relaxed. While the emphasis on the communal aspects of worshiping together has corrected some old abuses, it has certainly introduced some new ones. In most parish communities, the sense of majesty, holy awe, and fear of the Lord is gone. Many sanctuaries more closely resemble community meeting halls than a temple that houses God Himself. This loss of respect for the house of God has led to a loss of respect for the Eucharist itself. This lack of respect is demonstrated by a lack of holy decorum.

The loud talk, inappropriate laughter, improper dress, and lackadaisical participation through posture, piety, and verbal response that can be witnessed in many churches indicate how far we have slipped in respect of the Eucharist. Our physical demeanor reveals the attitude of our hearts. Conversely, developing a proper decorum toward the temple of God and the Holy Eucharist can help us cultivate a holy disposition and fervency of desire for the Real Presence. Modest and appropriate dress, speaking only when necessary and in hushed tones, genuflecting before entering the pew, kneeling with reverence, praying our liturgical responses with devotion and conviction, and making the Sign of the Cross or bowing before receiving the Eucharist all help us to keep our attention focused on the One who offers Himself to us in the form of bread and wine. Our body language, our style of dress, our tone of voice can all help or hinder the spiritual benefits we receive in Holy Communion.

A Living Faith: Hunger for the Eucharist

A living faith makes us hungry for the Eucharist because a living faith is fueled by the Eucharistic Presence. It is the food of our soul.

As we have discussed in so many other places, our human condition leaves us ripe for sin. Left on our own, the appetites of the flesh would eventually swallow us up. To remain faithful, we need the spiritual strength which comes only from the Eucharist. Father Reginald Garrigou-Lagrange puts it this way in his book *The Three Ages of the Interior Life:* "Our sensible appetites, inclined to sensuality and to sloth, need to be vivified by contact with the virginal body of Christ, who endured most frightful sufferings for love of us. We, who are always inclined to pride, to lack of consideration, to forgetfulness of the greatest truths, to spiritual folly, need to be illumined by contact with the sovereignly luminous intellect of the Savior, who is 'the way, the truth, and the life.'"[15]

What do we do if our "living faith" isn't very alive? The best remedy is to initiate a time of personal prayer through the use of Scripture. A daily dialogue with God centered on the Living Word helps us to become alive in Christ. In addition, we should practice the virtues and live the Beatitudes. Making daily sacrifices to God through prudent and temperate living, showing charity toward our neighbor, acting with courage and fortitude, and thanking God for all of His blessings stir up the gift of faith we received in Baptism. Our hunger for the Eucharist will grow and our faith will come alive, ignited by the fire of zeal.

Another way—and perhaps one of the best—to develop a hunger for the Eucharist is by making a proper thanksgiving after receiving our Lord. It is common everyday etiquette to thank someone for a favor received, and yet, how frequently we leave daily or Sunday Mass without so much as a nod in the direction of the One whom we have received. How this must wound the heart of Jesus! He gives Himself to us in an act of utter humility and love, and we barely acknowledge Him. Recall the parable of the ten lepers. After Jesus healed them, they all walked away. Only one returned to give thanks. He was the one to whom Jesus said, "Your faith has been your salvation." He was healed not only in body, but, more importantly, in spirit. His salvation was secured.

After receiving our Blessed Lord in Holy Communion, we need to thank Him for all that He has given us. Our gratitude could never exceed the measureless benefits we have received from His Eucharistic Presence, but He accepts our humble offering with gracious generosity and love. As true thanksgiving takes root in our hearts, so too does an ardent desire to receive the One who gives us every spiritual blessing in the heavens.

The Fruit of Ardent Desire and Spiritual Communion

A desire to be united to Jesus is the preeminent grace of the Eucharist. "In our inner life it is the Eucharist above all which expresses our personal union with Jesus.... The more perfectly we become assimilated to Christ in the Eucharist the more perfect will be our unity in him."[16]

Those who have mined the riches of Eucharistic treasure share that their lives are marked by a conscious anticipation for the Eucharist which is interwoven into the structure of the day. Often their minds turn toward the One whom they desire to receive. And, as their minds turn toward the Sacramental Presence of Jesus, flames of love stir the inner confines of their hearts. They experience an ever-increasing desire to be united to Jesus *all of the time.* This is the fruit of ardent desire, and it is produced by receiving Jesus in the Sacrament with fervency and spiritual effectiveness.

This holy desire to be continuously united to Jesus flows from the Eucharistic Presence into the soul that is properly disposed to receive Him. We become one with Him physically by receiving the host, and we become one with Him spiritually—in mind, heart, and affection. For this reason, the Fathers of the Church made a distinction between a sacramental reception and a spiritual reception of the Sacrament.[17] This distinction has led to the holy practice of making a *spiritual communion*, an act of love prompted by the ardent desire to receive Holy Communion even when we cannot.

No contact with Jesus is more efficacious for our spiritual lives than receiving Him physically through the Sacrament of the Eucharist. However, legitimate reasons can prevent us from doing so—the inability to attend Sunday Mass because of illness, inadvertently breaking the Eucharistic fast, a scheduling problem which makes daily Mass impossible. Each of these, for example, can keep us away from the Sacrament. And, even when we have received Jesus through the Sacrament, love for Him brings our minds back to Him many times during the day, fueling our desire for Him with anticipation and hope. In these cases, spiritual communion is a worthy and holy practice.

To make a spiritual communion, we simply unite ourselves with the One we love by fully turning our hearts and minds to Him. Picturing Him in His Sacramental Presence, viewing Him with our mind's eye in the monstrance, remembering the moment we received Him last—these are effective ways to direct our attention toward Jesus in the Eucharist. Then, we quietly tell Him of our love. We may spontaneously speak to Him from the fullness of our heart, or we may choose one of the formal prayers for spiritual communion. In either case, we experience abundant fruit from this act of love, and our hearts grow even warmer as we anticipate the next time we can receive Jesus sacramentally.

As we receive the Eucharist with humility, respect, living faith, and hunger, we will notice that our days become punctuated with constant reminders of God's love for us and His love for others. It is not that His involvement in our lives will have increased, but rather that our spiritual blindness will have been healed. We will experience the heart of God active within all of our circumstances of daily living. What is more, we will also discover that our own hearts have been transformed in the process. And in time, the prophetic words of Ezekiel will have come to pass in us: "I will give you a new heart and place a new spirit within you, taking from your bodies your stony hearts and giving you natural hearts.... You shall be my people, and I will be your God" (Ez 36:26, 28, NAB). Our hearts will have been transformed into the very heart of our Lord Jesus Christ.

Meeting With Jesus: Eucharistic Adoration

Ronald Lawlor, O.F.M. Cap., relates the story of how he came to appreciate the Real Presence of Jesus in the Eucharist while he was just a young child. He writes,

> *Among my first memories, from the time when I was only three or four, is the memory of how my mother helped me realize that Jesus is with us in the Eucharist.*
>
> *My mother used to take me for walks, but she did not walk past churches. Churches were for going into. She took me in, guided me all the way to the communion rail, and knelt to pray.*
>
> *I saw the earnestness with which her lips moved quietly, and felt the attention with which she listened to one I certainly could not see nor hear. Her whole heart was in her prayer. Obviously she was talking to someone important, though all I could see was the gold tabernacle and the flickering light near it.*
>
> *All this fascinated me, but not for long. After a short time, I had had enough. I pulled on her skirt. "Time to go." She seemed*

not even to hear me. So I said the same thing over and over, my voice gradually getting louder and louder.

Finally, we left. As we left, my mother told me: "That is where Jesus is." From the time I was a tiny infant, I am sure, before I understood anything, and through times when my understanding was most vague, she had spoken to me of Jesus, our Savior and our God.

Now if my mother said Jesus was right here (and she was very wise), and if Jesus said so himself: well, that was it. Catholic faith in the Eucharist had been proclaimed to me, and I knew it was true.

Later, when I did graduate work in psychology, I could spell out reasons why a child can feel sure of even the most astonishing things said by a parent. But when in theology I studied the nature and causes of faith I could see why even as a child my faith was not just a subjective "feeling sure," that might just disappear when more sophisticated wondering about the world began.

In this wonderful and fearful world, in which God really dwells, someone who had divine faith had spoken a truth of faith to a very small child. But it was a child who, in Baptism, had received the great gift of faith. Even then, without my knowing it, the Lord had given my small mind a preparedness to grasp as true the good things he wanted me to know. Now I knew one of the best things.[18]

How many children come to know about the Real Presence of Jesus in the Eucharist through the words spoken to them by a faith-filled mother or grandmother, father or grandfather? Faith is meant to be proclaimed. It is meant to be heard. And when it is heard, the grace of Baptism lays hold of it and truth grows and flourishes in the soul. So much so, that sometimes a vocation is forged in the most humble of moments.

But it is the faith of the mother that captivates my attention in this story. How much the Blessed Sacrament must have meant to this young woman, that she would take her three-year-old into every church she passed as they walked through the streets of town! Her love for Jesus, present in the tabernacle, is an inspiration to us all. Indeed, she knew the rich treasure of the Sacramental Presence of our Lord. And with faith and confidence, she made herself available to every spiritual blessing Jesus longed to give her.

Just as Jesus desires for us to take Him into our own bodies through reception of Holy Communion, so too does He want us to spend time with Him before His Eucharistic Presence. These personal encounters with Jesus help us to grow in faith and experience the abundant life He longs to give us. They become moments of transformation which imbue us with the Radiant Presence of Jesus Christ.

St. Paul writes these inspired words in 2 Corinthians 3:18: "And we all, with unveiled face, beholding the glory of the Lord, are being changed into his likeness from one degree of glory to another; for this comes from the Lord who is the Spirit." When we come with openness of heart to pray before the Eucharistic Presence of our Lord, whether He is reposed in the tabernacle or exposed in the monstrance, we grow more and more into His likeness. And the effects of this transformation are evident in every aspect of our life.

In the Presence of a Holy God

Our Holy Father, himself a man of deep prayer and Eucharistic adoration, has encouraged Catholics everywhere to seek the rich spiritual benefits available through this transforming Eucharistic worship. He writes,

Indeed, since the Eucharistic mystery was instituted out of love, and makes Christ sacramentally present, it is worthy of thanksgiving and worship.... The Church and the world have a great need of Eucharistic worship. Jesus waits for us in this Sacrament of love.

Let us be generous with our time in going to meet him in adoration and contemplation full of faith, and open to making amends for the serious offenses and crimes of the world. May our adoration never cease.[19]

In this statement, Pope John Paul II gives us three reasons to participate in Eucharistic adoration—to fulfill Jesus' request that we spend time with Him, to grow into His image and likeness, and to share in the work of redemption through reparation.

Enter Into the Holy Hour

Archbishop Fulton J. Sheen resolved on the day of his Ordination that he would spend an hour before the Blessed Sacrament every day. In his autobiography, he recounts the benefits of this daily Holy Hour. Among the benefits he mentions is the effect of Eucharistic adoration on his prayer life, his vocation, his victory over temptation, and his preaching. And he shares about miraculous events that happened in the lives of others who acquired this same practice through his encouragement. Consider this story:

A monsignor who, because of a weakness for alcohol and consequent scandal, was told to leave his parish went into another diocese on a trial basis, where he made my retreat. Responding to the grace of the Lord, he gave up alcohol, was restored to effectiveness in his priesthood, made the Holy Hour every day and died in the Presence of the Blessed Sacrament."[20]

Throughout the annals of Church history we find example upon example of the manifold blessings of God being poured out upon us through the Blessed Sacrament, the Heart of our Lord Jesus Christ. And through these blessings we radiate the Presence of Jesus Christ to the world.

How, then, do we make a Holy Hour and share in these blessings?

First and foremost, a Holy Hour is a time of prayer. As with any prayer time, we must first recollect ourselves, aware of what we intend to do (pray) and of whose Presence we are in. Next, we engage in the prayer itself. If we are unaccustomed to spending an entire hour in prayer, we may find it helpful at first to structure our Holy Hour. In chapter three, we examined the four intentions of heart that we should bring to prayer. These form the acronym ACTS—adoration, contrition, thanksgiving, and supplication. We might divide our hour into four equal parts, spending fifteen minutes on each of these intentions.

But, as we grow more comfortable in the Presence of the Blessed Sacrament, our time in prayer should gradually give over to a contemplation. A time of simply gazing into the face of the One whom we love. Just sitting quietly before the Radiant Splendor of Jesus Christ, allowing the rays of His love to penetrate into all areas of our hearts, offering our hearts to Him in quiet exchange for the One which He offers us, letting His presence transform us into His image and likeness—this should eventually make up the bulk of our time with Him. Our disposition should be one of listening, the ears of our hearts fastened to the mouth of God, ready to hear all that He has to say. "Speak, Lord, for your servant is listening," should be the words of our lips.

As it is with all prayer, there are times when it comes easily and times when it is more difficult. In dry times, we should especially offer our humble presence as a sacrifice of praise before the Blessed Sacrament in reparation for our sins and the sins of the world. In these moments, Jesus is simply asking us for our faithfulness. The words He spoke to His apostles in the Garden of Gethsemane ring clear for us as well: "Can you not spend one hour with me?"

Throughout the ages women of prayer have discovered the power of Eucharistic adoration. Even when we are busy or distracted, the great spiritual benefits gained from spending time with Jesus in the Blessed Sacrament transform us and revolutionize our lives. Adrienne von Speyer, a contemporary mystic, wife, mother, doctor, writes:

> *Lord, I want to thank you for your presence.... I want to thank you for being here, veiled in the mystery of the host, but so fully present that you yourself teach us to pray and help us to live. You are so fully present that we come to receive from you and take with us what your presence bestows upon us: certainty of faith, the love of your dwelling among us.*
>
> *Lord, you know how weak and distracted we are and how we consider everything else more important than you; but again and again you guide us back to this place where you dwell in order to change us.*[21]

As we gaze on the Lord's glory with unveiled faces, we are transformed into the very image of our Lord (see 2 Cor 3:18). Like Mary, our Mother, we can then carry the blessing of Jesus Christ to our families, our communities, our world.

Blessed Faustina Kowalska, whom Pope John Paul II has called "the great apostle of Divine Mercy in our time," prayed that Our Lord would make her a *living host,* hidden and broken to be given to others. In this way, she desired to imitate our Lord in His Eucharistic Presence. She begged, "Jesus, transform me, miserable and sinful as I am, into your own self.... Transform me in Yourself, O Jesus, that I may be a living sacrifice and pleasing to You.... All the good that is in me is due to Holy Communion. I owe everything to it. I feel this holy fire has transformed me completely. Oh, how happy I am to be a dwelling for You, O Lord! My heart is a temple in which You dwell continually."[22]

Jesus desires that each of us become a temple in which He dwells continually. He desires that through reception of Holy Eucharist and moments spent before His Blessed Sacrament we might be transformed into His very image and likeness, filled with the fire of His very life. Impregnated with His divine love, we will imbue the world with the fragrance of Jesus Christ in power and in grace.

The Healing Power of the Eucharist

Those involved in ministry speak time and again of magnificent healings that have taken place through the Eucharistic Presence— healings of mind, body, and spirit. In every case, interaction with Jesus of Nazareth, present in the Sacred Species, is a life-changing event that brings transformation and new life.

Consider, for example, the two famous physical cures that took place at Lourdes after the Blessing of the Sick with the Blessed Sacrament. Both involved the healing of a laborer who had experienced multiple injuries and could not walk. One was Gabriel Gargam from France (1901) and the other was Jack Traynor from England (1923). Gargam's healing happened at the Blessing of the Sick a few hours after he had received Holy Communion. When he received the Eucharist, he experienced overwhelming graces and a spiritual cure. This eventually led to his physical healing later in the day. Traynor's healing began to take place as he bathed in the waters at Lourdes. The healing was completed when the priest made the Sign of the Cross over him with the Blessed Sacrament. Many conversions took place as a result of these cures.[23]

Recently, a priest friend told me about miraculous healings that took place during a Mass he celebrated for a Spanish-speaking congregation. During his homily, Father preached about the healing power of the Eucharist. He exhorted the assembly to trust in God's love. As he was preaching, a young English-speaking girl who was suffering with a serious throat condition excitedly asked her friend what Father was saying. She told her friend that while Father was speaking, she felt a warm hand touch her throat and her pain had completely disappeared. Later, it was confirmed that, indeed, her throat condition was healed.

At this same Mass was a man suffering with four bleeding ulcers. He was scheduled to have surgery. As he received the Eucharist, he felt a penetrating warmth fill his stomach. He immediately believed he was being healed. When he went to his doctor for his preoperative visit a couple of days later, no trace of the ulcers could be found.

Two other individuals who attended the Mass reported that their thyroid conditions were healed. Stories like these encourage our faith and trust in God's love for us. They also give us a deeper love and appreciation for Jesus, who comes to us in the humble form of bread and wine.

But, while God desires to heal us physically, His ultimate concern is for our spiritual condition. For what does physical health merit us if we are doomed to spiritual death? It is the impurity of our soul that God longs to cleanse with the Blood of His Son, Jesus Christ. It is the pain of our hearts that God desires to mitigate through the love of His Son. It is the infirmity of our spirit that God wants to heal through the restorative power of the Holy Eucharist.

Father Benedict Groeschel provides us with a profound story of one man's conversion to God through the Eucharist at the moment of his death. Father Groeschel writes:

I brought Holy Communion as Viaticum to a repentant man who had in the past rejected Christ, hated the Church, involved himself in the gay scene with abandon and debauchery. According to his own account he had rejected his baptism and faith, hated and cursed the Church and all the Church stood for, and when the Holy Spirit called to him shortly before the end, with tears of repentance and joyous gratitude, he embraced the death that sexual indulgence had caused. The Son of God (who had been made the Son of man in the womb of the Virgin Mother) came to him at the end of his wasted life and he embraced Christ. He acknowledged that the little wafer I put on his tongue as he lay dying was the same Jesus of Nazareth who summoned the good thief to paradise at the hour of death.[24]

Through the gift of the Holy Eucharist, Jesus makes available to us His own Most Sacred Heart, the very heart that was pierced with a sword upon Calvary's hill. He gives us His Heart so that our own hearts might be purified and cleansed, strengthened and made new, healed and set free. As Groeschel closes his story, he states, "It is a mystery to me that any person who claims that he or she accepts the Catholic faith and knows this does not fall down on his or her face before the Eucharist and cry out, 'Jesus, Savior, have mercy on me a sinner.'"[25]

How do *we* respond to the Eucharistic Presence—do we see and believe in its power? Jesus longs that we might meet Him in the Eucharist as our Divine Physician, our Purifier, our Comforter, our Healer.

Our Lord desires that we, like the legendary Longinus, believe in the power of His Holy Blood so that the spiritual blindness of our souls might give way to spiritual sight. He wants to mitigate our doubts and reservations, insecurities and fears—like those of the Basilian monk—through His own Flesh and Blood.

Just as He ministered to Archbishop Fulton Sheen, God longs to invigorate our life's vocation through His own life exposed to us in the Blessed Sacrament. And just as He healed the two men at Lourdes, and the four people at the Mass my friend celebrated, Jesus may choose to heal the infirmities of our bodies, that we might gain spiritual strength through the gift of faith.

Most especially, Jesus longs to purify and cleanse us—just like the man dying of AIDS or the monsignor healed of alcoholism. He wants to set us free from the sin that holds us in bondage, and heal the wounds of our lives that torment our souls and plague our hearts. We have only to receive Him in His Eucharistic Presence, unite ourselves to Him during the day through spiritual communion, and adore Him in the Most Blessed Sacrament to experience the transformative effects of His love.

Let us go before the Eucharistic Presence of Jesus Christ with faith and confidence. Let us drink deeply of Jesus Christ, our Lord and Savior, our Redeemer and Healer, our Courage and our Strength. Let us drink deeply from the Fountain of living waters. Let us taste and see the goodness of the Lord. Let us be a Eucharistic People who are transformed by the Body and Blood of Jesus Christ and bear His presence to the world!

It is fitting that as we close this chapter on the great gift of the Eucharist, we should join ourselves to Jesus Christ through spiritual communion:

Act of Spiritual Communion

My Jesus, I believe that You are in
the Blessed Sacrament.
I love You above all things, and
I long for You in my soul.
Since I cannot now receive You sacramentally,
come at least spiritually into my heart.
As though You have already come,
I embrace You and unite myself
entirely to You;
never permit me to be separated from you.[26]

Resurrection: Made New for the Abundant Life

*T*hroughout the course of this book we have discussed the holy mission that God has given to us as women in the world today. Through His Holy Catholic Church, He has asked us to aid humanity in not falling and to be the healers of the world. To accomplish this divine task, God bestows upon us *every spiritual blessing in the heavens.* We begin to consciously experience these "*spiritual blessings*" as our lives are conformed to His holy will.

Healing for the Wounded Heart

If we are to fulfill our mission, there is one spiritual blessing in particular that we must receive: the grace of healing. Every time we sin and each time a sin is committed against us, it inflicts a wound to the heart. Like so many tiny knives tearing at the delicate fiber of our being, the sharp and pointed assault of personal sin and sins committed against us render our hearts leaky vessels out of which runs the tender love of our merciful God. God pours His love, His mercy, His grace into our hearts—they, in turn, leak it out through the sievelike openings of injury and affliction.

But our God is the Divine Physician, and with ultimate gentleness He desires to suture the wounds of our hearts with the finest threads of grace. Like a rich and lustrous brocade shimmering with silver and gold, our hearts become distinguished vessels dedicated and useful to God for the most noble of service (see 2 Tm 2:20-21).

Through the ministry of *Living His Life Abundantly* I have spoken to thousands of people. In the letters I receive, through telephone conversations and media interviews, at conferences and during retreats, people have shared their pain, their tribulations, and the struggles of their souls with me. They have also shared some of their deepest and most intimate wounds of the heart. I have heard stories of incest and rape. Stories of molestation and sexual abuse. Stories of abandonment and neglect. Stories of emotional and psychological trauma. Many others have told me of heart-wrenching efforts to mitigate the effects of sinful decisions they have made in the past—decisions of abortion, adultery, sterilization. Choices of promiscuity, homosexuality, alcohol and drug abuse. Choices which have grieved others—friends, parents, spouses, children.

Though some of the situations shared with me are impossible to resolve by human standards, time and again I have witnessed the healing power of Jesus Christ setting His people free from bondage, free from the effects of past sins, free from years of painful memories. Like the Resurrection of Jesus on that first Easter morning, new life rises from death, and hope springs from ashes. People are made new by the healing love of Jesus Christ. However, before the healing takes place we must cooperate fully with the grace God is giving. We must admit our need for healing, desire to be healed, and participate in the sacraments of new birth—Penance and Eucharist. The story of Tina illustrates what can happen when a person cooperates with God in this way.

As a young girl, Tina was told that she was an "unplanned baby." Feeling unwanted by her parents, she desired only to please them. However, nothing she could do won their approval. She was a gawky and awkward child whose lack of coordination often made her the subject of ridicule by her mother; her father's emotional coldness made her feel inadequate and incomplete. Tina made her way through her first few years of life feeling insecure and unloved. Though she excelled in school and enjoyed childhood playmates and classroom friendships, something deep inside of her was missing. The area of her heart that God intended to be filled with parental love and approval was a gaping hole.

Perhaps it wasn't surprising when, at age eight, Tina began to respond to the attentions of a male cousin, her senior by ten years. He made her feel special and wanted. Confusing his attention for love and his sexual overtures for affection, she gave in to his sinful actions, not fully comprehending what was happening. When his assaults became more demanding and more brutal, she began to feel increasingly uncomfortable and afraid. Finally, he and his family moved away, freeing her from his nightmarish abuse.

Though the molestation continued for less than a year, this wound to Tina's heart plagued her through her teenage years and on into adulthood. She entered her adolescent years believing that the only way for her to gain approval or acceptance was through sexual activity. She pursued this line of thinking and its subsequent pattern of behavior throughout her young adult years.

Tina brought this unhealed wound of her heart into her marriage, where it continued to produce bitter fruit. She had a chronic problem with fidelity, and yet she dreaded the prospect of her husband discovering her duplicity, for she was most afraid of losing her family. This breach of the marriage covenant, added to the painful memories of sexual abuse and years of disgust for her own sinful actions, were crippling her spiritually and emotionally. She was distrustful of others, constantly questioning their motives, and she rushed to judgment when things did not go her way. She often felt manipulated and used in personal and professional relationships.

In spite of all of this, Tina was a practicing Catholic. Spiritually, she was tormented by the hypocritical nature of her life. She had begun to dread Sunday Mass and found herself making excuses for not attending with her family. This only complicated the guilt and pain she felt. She knew she should go to the Sacrament of Reconciliation, but she didn't believe it could possibly change things. Besides, she knew from past history that she would confess her sins only to commit them again in the near future. She was close to despair and felt that nothing could help her.

One morning she was waiting with her children at the bus stop. A woman she knew from her parish struck up a conversation with her, told her about an upcoming retreat, and asked her if she'd like to go. Knowing she had to do something about her current circumstances, Tina accepted the invitation in a desperate attempt to put her life back in order.

Identifying the Wounds of Our Hearts

Because we live in a fallen world, all of us have been sinned against by others. Not all wounds of the heart involve sexual molestation or feeling unwanted by parents, but each of us has been injured in some way. Hateful comments, prejudicial remarks, losing someone close to us, the betrayal of a friend or spouse, unrequited love—in all of these ways, hurt and confusion sting the heart with razorlike precision.

After the initial pain subsides, we most typically categorize these experiences as "the way life is," and, in time, we go on about our business. But some of the injuries cut so deeply they have a long-term effect on us. Our memory stores these pains—sometimes in the conscious mind, sometimes in the subconscious—and, like an unchecked virus making its way through the body, these stored memories begin to produce ugly symptoms in our lives.

This was the case with Tina. Though Tina came to the retreat knowing she needed to put her life back in order, she did not know the root cause of her current circumstances. For example, she blamed her marital infidelity on the workaholic nature of her husband and her subsequent loneliness. And she thought the lack of trust she felt toward others, with its accompanying sense of manipulation, came from being passed over for promotions in her place of work.

Five Questions to Help You Identify the Source of Your "Wounds"

I have found the following five questions to be effective in discovering areas that need to be healed in my own life as well as in the lives of others. One or more may indicate a need for inner healing. We might say these are the possible symptoms of a "spiritual virus."

1. Do I find myself repeating the same sin over and over again? Tina was constantly confessing infidelity, for example. While there were areas in her marriage that certainly needed to be addressed, she knew she loved her husband. What caused her to be unfaithful, then? This was the question she needed to explore.

2. Is there an unhealthy pattern of behavior or pattern of thought that recurs in my life?

Have you ever heard yourself say things like...

- "No one likes me."
- "I get defensive every time I am questioned by someone in authority."
- "I go ___ (to the mall, to a movie, or some other favorite escape) every time I have to make a decision."

When we find that our physical and mental reactions remain constant in similar situations, and when these reactions are not healthy, this can signal a deeply rooted problem.

3. Do I overreact (either externally or internally) in some types of situations?

If our response to a certain situation is stronger than what most other people seem to experience in the same situation, a red flag should go up. The questions we must ask ourselves are, "What is stimulating such a strong response? What am I feeling? In what memory or event in my life could this emotion be rooted?"

In Tina's case, every time her husband smiled at her in a certain way, it reminded her of a facial expression of the cousin who had molested her. Her heart would quicken, anger would rise up within, and she would lash out at her surprised husband.

4. Do I walk around with a cloud over my head—a cloud of fear or anxiety, gloom and doom, depression or tension? Or, do I often feel like nothing can make me happy?

While there are some chemical and medical reasons that can cause these emotions (and these should be clinically evaluated), often the root cause of these symptoms is a wound of the heart.

Recently, a woman shared with me her experience of being

released from a feeling of shame related to events that took place in her early adult years. Though she had confessed and repented of her sin, she could not shake the feeling of doom that hung about her. Through the pastoral counseling of a holy priest schooled in inner healing, she discovered that the shame was a symptom of a wound of the heart. The priest's intercessory prayer, her honesty, and the Blessed Eucharist healed her of the injury and released her from the shame and gloom which had characterized her daily life.

5. Have I exhausted the natural and the spiritual means of dealing with the problem, and still found that nothing has helped?

We read in Sirach, "Hold the physician in honor, for he is essential to you, and God it was who established his profession" (Sir 38:1, NAB). When we find ourselves depressed, obsessed by thoughts, ridden with compulsive behaviors, or dealing with severe emotional and psychological issues, it is always best for us to seek the wise counsel of a physician or mental health professional. Many problems are symptomatic of a hormone imbalance, chemical imbalance, or physical sickness.

In addition, we should avail ourselves of the sacraments, seek prayer and discernment, and talk openly and honestly with a spiritual director. However, when we have tried all of these means and the problem remains, it may indicate the need for inner healing.

In Tina's case, her answers to these five questions began to alert her to the possibility that more was troubling her than loneliness and work-related issues. Though she was somewhat concerned about what she would discover, she decided to go for individual prayer the first night of the retreat to see if she could discover the source of her wounded heart. When she met with the spiritual director and told her she suspected that something was deeply troubling her, the spiritual director gently probed Tina's memory to uncover the root cause of her problem. Tina candidly answered the questions she was asked.

First, the spiritual director asked her when all of this began. As she thought about it, Tina discovered that her defensiveness, sense of manipulation, and promiscuity had a long history. In fact, it was hard for her to remember a time when all of it was not part of her life. The spiritual director asked her if she could remember her childhood and if it was happy or sad. Tina immediately responded that it was a sad childhood. There were happy moments, of course, but it was sad most of all.

Next, the spiritual director asked her why it was a sad childhood. As she remembered back, Tina's attention was immediately focused on the time of her molestation.

"Is this when you first became sad as a child?" the spiritual director gently asked.

"No," was Tina's reply. "It preceded this time."

With patience and concern the spiritual director continued to lead Tina back through those early childhood years. Ultimately, Tina came to realize that the sense of being unwanted as a child was the overwhelming sadness of her life. Though it had been hidden to her, this sense of neglect and abandonment influenced many of the decisions she made. Unfortunately, these choices often led to further rejection, pain, hurt, and confusion. For Tina, this revelation, though painful in itself, was liberating and transforming.

Once the root cause was exposed, the spiritual director led Tina in a prayer which asked Jesus to heal the wound itself and free her from all its effects. Jesus Christ, who is the same yesterday, today, and forever, can heal the torments of our heart just as He healed people when He walked on the earth two thousand years ago. Asking Him to enter into our painful memories and touch our interior injuries with His healing love is what inner healing is all about. In inner healing God reveals in the light of truth what has been hidden in the darkness of our hearts. We then prayerfully ask Him to heal and bind the ill effects of the wounds which we have suffered.

Through the prayer for inner healing, Tina began to experience the spiritual blessings God had in store for her that weekend. She felt an interior freedom which she had never experienced. For the first time, Tina allowed herself to believe that God loved her into life and that no matter what her parents had thought about the circumstances of her birth, God desired her, wanted her, fashioned her after His own heart. She came to see that even in that dark moment of sexual molestation, God had not abandoned her. His love was with her even though her abuser exercised his free will in a way that flouted the laws of God. And now, at a time preordained by God, He wanted her healing process to begin. God only sought her permission to begin to peel the layers of hurt, the layers of pain, the layers of trauma from the depths of her heart.

Tina also learned that God wanted to heal her from the effects of her own personal sin. He wanted her to "be holy and blameless in his sight," filled with grace, like the Mother of His Son. He would give her the ability to live out this call to grace; all she had to do was accept it. She discovered that no sin is greater than the mercy of God.

God's love is an infinite ocean from which He wants us to drink. The Sacrament of Reconciliation is a font of this mercy; when we receive this sacrament with a repentant heart, God not only forgives us, but He also forgets the sins we have committed.

Convicted of His love, Tina made her way to the Sacrament of Reconciliation to experience the healing waters of forgiveness.

Obstacles to Inner Healing

Jesus came that we might have life and have it more abundantly (see Jn 10:10). And yet, we have seen that the sins committed against us as well as our own personal sin put us in spiritual bondage. This captivity prevents us from experiencing the fullness of life that God has intended for us from all eternity.

God desires that each of us be set free from all that imprisons us. What, then, prevents the wounds of our hearts from being healed? These reasons are many and varied, but here are some of the most common.

1. We do not admit we need this healing.

One obstacle to healing is not admitting there is a problem. Many people refuse to admit that the traumas they have experienced in life have wounded them in any way. This is a pity because, as we have seen, ignoring the problem doesn't make it go away.

Any spiritual virus plaguing our souls will eventually produce unhealthy symptoms in our lives. These symptoms take a variety of forms, some of which we have discussed; others include anger, bitterness, resentment, maliciousness, an inability to love or receive love, rebellion, callousness, a sense of worthlessness. These symptoms cripple us from realizing the fullness of life that God wants for us. They also affect our attitude toward life, which can become a source of pain for those around us.

2. We do not want to be healed.

There are some individuals who come for healing prayer but never intend to give up their suffering. I remember a man who came to me for inner healing. He had been deeply wounded by the rejection of his wife. His attitude toward her was bitter and hateful. He claimed he wanted to be healed of the pain in his heart and put his life back together again. But through the course of weeks that I prayed with him, it became obvious he relished his bitterness and wielded it like a cudgel of revenge against his wife. His hatred had become his life's fuel. Not only did he not want to be healed, but he was rejecting the grace God was giving him by his sinful and vindictive actions.

Still others reject healing because they like the attention created by their problem. Agnes was such a person. She had grown up in an alcoholic home, which had deeply scarred her. Even though she was well aware of the negative effects her childhood had produced in her life and could identify areas where healing was needed, and even though she prayed for healing in those areas, she did not want to be healed. She liked the attention she received from those who prayed with her.

Unless we truly desire to be healed, all of the prayers in the world will be of no avail, because we erect a wall of resistance that prevents God's healing love from entering.

3. We do not exercise our faith.

Sometimes we are tempted to think that our problems are bigger than God, or that God doesn't want to heal us. Not only is this a sin of presumption, but such attitudes prevent us from experiencing the freedom God intends for us.

If our faith is weak, we need to ask God to increase it. Recall the words Jesus spoke to the father who brought his possessed son to Him, asking Jesus to help him if He could. Jesus responded, "All things are possible to him who believes."

The father then replied, "I believe; help my unbelief!" (Mk 9:23-24).

When our faith is weak, we need to recall this passage from Sacred Scripture and pray that our belief and trust in God's power will increase. One way that we can encourage our faith is to read through the stories of healing in the New Testament. As we come to see the compassion of Jesus, His love for the weak and infirm, our faith and trust grows stronger.

Jesus is the same yesterday, today, and forever. He longs to heal us, just as He healed the many people who sought His help two thousand years ago. These stories remind us of a tender and merciful Savior who longs to bring the abundant life to His people. For, as Scripture tells us, "All things are possible with God" (Mk 10:27).

4. God wants us to offer up our suffering for a greater good.
While we will be discussing this in the next chapter, it is important to understand here that God wants us to attach our sufferings to the Passion and death of Jesus Christ. United to the sufferings of Christ, our own struggles become a source of our Lord's redemptive grace that flows into the lives and hearts of His people. However, this does not mean that we do not pray for healing—physical, emotional, or spiritual. We must believe that God's will for us is to be healed unless there is some very clear indication that it isn't.

This being said, some people are called to a special charism or gift called "redemptive suffering."[1] In these cases, God uses illness for a good greater than the benefit healing would provide. Throughout the history of the Church, many saints have been called to be a "victim soul" for the sake of the kingdom of God. By uniting their sufferings and wounds of the heart to the wounded heart of Christ, their trials become a source of grace and healing in the world.

Seen in this light, suffering is not so much an obstacle to healing as it is a special call or ministry. A person who has been called to a ministry of redemptive suffering responds to her pain with characteristic joy. Happiness lights her face, patience overrides her discomfort, and kindness marks her interactions with others. She is a source of grace to those around her. But unless we know that God has called us to this mission, we should pray for healing if it be God's will.

5. We fail to respond to God's grace.

The spiritual life is a cooperative enterprise between God and us. He gives us the grace, but we must use it. This applies as much to the grace of healing as to any other grace that God gives us.

Some individuals sabotage their own healing process by engaging in activities, thinking processes, or situations that are certain to compromise the rich treasure of healing God has bestowed upon them. I can remember praying with a man once who had a terrible problem with pornography. This was rooted in some deep-seated wounds of the heart for which we were praying. Little progress was made, until one day he shared with me that his route to work took him through a part of town notorious for its girlie-bars and pornography stores. The temptation they posed was too great for him.

When this situation was revealed, so was the solution. The very next day he changed his route to work, thereby removing the obstacle that had impeded his wounded and troubled heart from receiving the grace that God was giving.

Another example of the interaction between God's grace and

our response to it can be found in Tina's story. Cooperating with the grace God gave her during the retreat weekend was absolutely essential for Tina's continued healing. As the weekend came to a close, it was obvious from her radiant expression that she was filled with new life. Transformation had begun to take place in her, but it needed to be nurtured and strengthened. Filled with hope and anticipation, Tina was ready to go home to her family and begin to write a new chapter in their family history. However, she knew that serious temptation awaited her.

First, there would be the assault of doubt that would come at her. Had she really experienced the healing touch of God? Next, she would have to break off her current extramarital affair. Would she have the courage to do it? Finally, the old memories and hurts of the past would come back to haunt her. Was she spiritually equipped to fight them?

With the help of the spiritual director, Tina worked out a reasonable plan to cooperate with the healing grace she had received. She committed herself to a time of prayer every day. Given her schedule, she knew that mornings would be best. She put it on her daily calendar, just as she would any other important event for the day.

Then, Tina made a decision to attend daily Mass as frequently as she could. She knew that she needed to be strengthened through the Eucharist. Tina also determined to go to the Sacrament of Reconciliation as often as possible and no less than once a month. Having experienced the healing grace of this sacrament, she was aware of its profound effect.

Next, Tina decided to spend time with Jesus in the Blessed Sacrament. Some wounds are so deep that God in His mercy heals them gradually, layer by layer. As we spend time before the Eucharistic Presence, we are bathed in the light of the One whose Blood redeems us and sets us free.

Tina also decided to get involved with other people who were striving for holiness and healing. Christian community is essential if we are going to make progress in the spiritual life. She knew that her own parish had a prayer group that met weekly. She decided to attend that very week.

Finally, Tina had seen for herself how deeply rooted was the wound of her heart. She promised to seek the help and assistance of a Christian counselor and spiritual director. If we are going to grow in holiness we must admit the truth about ourselves as revealed to us by God and the insights of others.

Tina knew that to follow through on these commitments would involve sacrifice. But she also knew that the benefits would far outweigh her effort. God can never be outdone in generosity.

6. Sometimes we are not healed because we harbor unforgiveness in our hearts.

Because of the magnitude of this final obstacle, we will consider it in a separate section.

Lack of Forgiveness: The Greatest Obstacle of All

The thirty-something man approached me with tears in his eyes. It was almost the end of a long day in a southwestern city where I was giving a day of recollection to people involved in ministry.

"You really got me with what you just talked about," he said. "I've listened all day waiting to hear that special word you said our Lord would speak to each one of us. And I think I've just heard it."

The day had been divided into three segments—the lay person's mission in evangelizing the world today; the universal call to holiness; and overcoming obstacles in our mission as lay Catholics. In the third session, I had discussed, among other things, the obstacle of an unforgiving heart. It was in this session that the thirty-something man heard a word for him.

In the few minutes that we shared together, he told me about a family member who had caused great difficulty for himself and others in the family. "I haven't forgiven this person for the harm he caused. I lose my temper with him and I'm stressed out most of the time. I'm developing blood pressure problems and my anger is affecting my work. You said God says we must forgive. I don't think I can do it, but I want to try."

While the details of this man's story were unique, I certainly could relate to what he was saying. I remembered when I first heard the Lord's voice prompting me to forgive. Like the thirty-something man, I, too, was faced with forgiving someone who had caused me great torment. My decision to forgive began a process that has lasted most of my life.

But God's word on the subject of forgiveness is clear—and no person, circumstance, or situation is exempted:

> *Then Peter came up and said to him, "Lord, how often shall my brother sin against me, and I forgive him? As many as seven times?"*
>
> *Jesus said to him, "I do not say to you seven times, but seventy times seven."*
>
> MATTHEW 18:21-22

> *For if you forgive men their trespasses, your heavenly Father also will forgive you; but if you do not forgive men their trespasses, neither will your Father forgive your trespasses.*
>
> MATTHEW 6:14

Be merciful, even as your Father is merciful. Judge not and you will not be judged; condemn not, and you will not be condemned; forgive, and you will be forgiven; give, and it will be given to you; good measure, pressed down, shaken together, running over, will be put into your lap. For the measure you give will be the measure you get back.

LUKE 6:36-38

So if you are offering your gift at the altar, and there remember that your brother has something against you, leave your gift there before the altar and go; first be reconciled to your brother, and then come and offer your gift.

MATTHEW 5:23-24

You have heard that it was said, "You shall love your neighbor and hate your enemy." But I say to you, Love your enemies and pray for those who persecute you.... For if you love those who love you, what reward have you? ... You, therefore, must be perfect, as your heavenly Father is perfect.

MATTHEW 5:43-48

For the disciples of Jesus who first heard these words, they were indeed hard words to take. This was not the law of retribution that they knew as a people and a culture. Their forefathers had taught them a different law—"an eye for an eye, a tooth for a tooth."

Jesus' message of forgiveness was difficult for the disciples to receive for another reason as well. They had not yet witnessed the tremendous love and mercy of God revealed through the Passion, death, and resurrection of His only begotten Son, Jesus Christ. It is in the Paschal Mystery that we most vividly see the unconditional mercy of God. Through our Baptism, God's own mercy takes up residence within us in the form of sanctifying grace. Each time we avail ourselves of the Sacrament of Reconciliation, we experience anew the mercy of God.

That thirty-something man at the day of recollection knew he was incapable of forgiveness. What he needed to know was that he could forgive through the mercy of God active within him. Only by dispensing the mercy of God we have received can we begin to forgive others.

Each of us has experienced trauma, pain, humiliation, and abuse through the actions of others. Our hearts are bruised many times over in our lives. But God tells us we must forgive, and from the passages we have quoted we can see why. Our own salvation is intimately connected to the action of forgiveness. Jesus tells us that if we do not forgive, we will not be forgiven. If we judge and condemn, we too will be judged and condemned. The measure we measure with will be measured back to us. Lack of forgiveness brings an eternal sentence upon us—a sentence we create and one that begins in this life.

St. Paul tells us: "Be angry but do not sin; do not let the sun go down on your anger, and give no opportunity to the devil" (Eph 4:26-27). When we refuse to forgive, we sin. And through sin we choose evil over the grace of God. By so choosing, we make room for the devil to work within us, and the fruit of his labor is bitterness, resentment, hatred, and hostility. As we nurse these ill effects with the milk of sustained anger, they ultimately mature and alienate us from God. Like a twisting vine, they wrap around our heart, choking off the life of God within us. Left to itself, our soul becomes hard and stony, an impenetrable fortress of iron. We are imprisoned within ourselves, feeding on our anger as cancer feeds upon its host.

And the effects are profound. Like my thirty-something friend, our health often betrays our interior condition. Ulcers, blood pressure problems, and decreased memory skills are manifested. Cynicism, sarcasm, and vehemence spew from our mouths. Intolerance, agitation, short-temperedness mark our behavior. Clinical depression, a mental health problem largely caused by pent-up anger, becomes a real possibility.[2] We are miserable, and we make those around us miserable as well. Our lives become a living hell. Jesus tells us we must forgive because an unforgiving heart holds us in bondage. We become a prisoner of our own making.[3]

What, Then, Does It Mean to Forgive?

First, we must know what forgiveness is not.

> *To forgive does not mean that we condone the hurtful behavior.*
> *To forgive does not mean that our pain doesn't matter.*
> *To forgive does not mean that everything is OK.*
> *To forgive does not mean that I should allow ill will toward me to continue.*
> *To forgive does not mean that I should stay in an abusive situation.*
> *To forgive does not mean that I feel forgiveness.*

Rather, forgiveness is a free-will action, prompted by grace, which sets us free from the consequence of sin. In Matthew 18:18 we read, "Truly, I say to you, whatever you bind on earth shall be bound in heaven, and whatever you loose on earth shall be loosed in heaven." When we forgive, the harm committed against us loses its power over us. Anger flees, and with it go hostility, hatred, resentment, and bitterness. The wall of resistance that we have built around our hearts begins to crumble and fall. No longer held captive to the effects of anger, our stony hearts become "hearts of flesh." We are set free—and so is the person who has been held in spiritual bondage by the fetters of our unforgiveness.

How, Then, Do We Begin to Forgive—Especially When the Wrong Committed Against Us Is Deep and Painful?

Our thirty-something friend gives us the first step. We must *want* to forgive. Forgiveness is a matter of the will, not the heart. We choose to forgive; we decide to forgive. Feelings have nothing to do with it.

Sometimes the pattern of anger is so entrenched or the pain is so deep that we cannot make this decision. In these instances, we need to pray for the desire to forgive. If even praying for the desire to forgive is uncomfortable for us, we need to pray for the *desire to desire* to forgive. We take it back as far as we need to take it until we reach a certain assurance that we can begin at that point—and then we work our way forward, one desire at a time.

Our prayer might begin, *Lord I pray for the desire to desire to forgive. Help me to act through the power of your mercy in this situation.*

Eventually, we will find ourselves praying, *Lord, I pray for the desire to forgive. Thank You for demonstrating the power of Your mercy in me. Help me to forgive completely.*

And then, *Lord, I pray to forgive this person. Through Your mercy get me to the point where I can forgive completely.*

And finally, *Lord, I forgive. Thank You for Your faithfulness which has brought me to this point.*

It is important for us to remember that forgiveness is a process and it occurs one step at a time.[4]

How Can We Progress in This Action of Mercy?

Jesus gives us the answer to this question in Matthew 5:44: "*Pray for those who persecute you.*" As we enter into prayer for those who have hurt us, a dynamic begins to take place deep within our souls. We find that gradually, little by little, the pain we have experienced is assuaged and the anger we hold against that individual becomes tempered. Almost imperceptibly, we begin to experience God's love for that person. We enter into the mercy of God active within us and extend that mercy to our persecutor. In a sense, through our prayer, God uses us as an instrument of mercy in the life of the person who has wounded us.

How can we pray for our persecutors when their action against us has been so hurtful? I have found it useful to remember that at the moment the person was committing the injury, he (or she) could not have known God's love. Had that person known the extent of God's love—how much God loves each one of us—that person never could have committed the action.

During His crucifixion, Jesus begged His Father to forgive His murderers, "for they do not know what they do." Through ignorance or their own hurt and injury, our persecutors have been prevented from accepting the love and mercy of God that forever flows from the Sacred Heart of Jesus.

Indeed, then, our persecutor deserves our compassion. Through our intercessory prayer, we can help to heal the breach in that person's heart and prepare that person to receive the love of Jesus Christ. I think of the Good Thief hanging beside Jesus on Calvary. Scripture recounts that he jeered and mocked Jesus just like those around him (see Mt 27:44). But when the Good Thief recognized Jesus as the Messiah, his heart was changed (see Lk 23:40-42). Our prayers for our persecutors can help to bring them to this same recognition.

Can we recover from the hurt we have experienced?
Yes. Yes. Yes.
But, like forgiveness, recovery is also a choice. We must embrace the desire to be healed of our hurt, and seek this healing through the means that God gives us. For some, this may mean professional counseling. For others, it may mean time spent with a spiritual director. And for others, it may be a lifelong process that is

approached with the rising sun each day. In all cases, daily prayer and frequent reception of the Holy Eucharist and the Sacrament of Reconciliation are of ultimate importance.

I have also found that meditating on the Passion of Jesus is a wonderful source of healing. In St. Mark's account of Christ's Passion, we see many words that describe the intense emotional pain that Jesus experienced. Some of these words are *betrayed, filled with fear, sorrow to the point of death, deserted, manhandled, mocked, beaten, scourged, forsaken.*

Was there a pain or humiliation that Jesus did not suffer? Could there have been any emotion left untouched by His Passion? Was there one indignity He did not experience? As we meditate on the Passion of Jesus, we discover that every pain, hurt, and sorrow we have suffered was taken to the cross with Him. And His blood has redeemed it. We have only to appropriate the grace He merited for us.

Two Stories of the Power of Forgiveness

God has created the human person as a triune being who consists of body, mind, and spirit. Because we are an interrelated trinity, what affects one area of our being directly impacts other aspects of our makeup as well. For example, the interior condition of our soul can influence both our state of mind and our physical well-being. This is what my thirty-something friend discovered in his life. As he held on to unforgiveness, the bitterness and resentment it produced within him created blood pressure problems and reduced his productivity on the job.

However, when we cooperate with the grace God gives us to restore those areas of our spirit that have been damaged by our own sin or wounded by the sin of others, we often experience improved physical and mental health. Two stories experienced by people involved in the ministry of healing exemplify the healing effects of forgiveness. One involves a near drowning. The other is about a man in a spinal cord injury ward.

The Wound That Wouldn't Heal

Bill was a rough-and-tumble kind of guy. From the moment he came to the spinal cord injury ward, it was clear that his life was characterized by hard living. A truck driver by profession, he had been riding his motorcycle one night when a semi pushed him off the road and sent him and his Harley Sportster flying over an embankment.

His back was broken, which left him alive but a paraplegic. His lungs became badly infected by cinders he had ingested at the scene. Antibiotics had not cleared the infection.

Because of his spinal cord injury, he developed pressure sores on his back from not being turned often enough as he lay in bed. One sore was about seven inches wide and so deep that his spinal column was clearly visible. All nonsurgical attempts to close the sore had failed, and because of his infected lungs, surgery was not an option.

The prognosis was not good. In fact, Bill was dying. Each day, the medical staff would x-ray his lungs to see if they were clear enough to operate. And each day, the infection persisted.

Bill was in the intensive care unit when my friend, a mental health counselor who believs in the power of prayer, was assigned to his case. He first saw Bill strapped to a special bed that rotated him every few minutes. Knowing the severity of the man's condition, my friend asked Bill if he would like to pray. Bill agreed but admitted that he hadn't prayed in years. As my friend led him in prayer, he sensed that there was more at work in Bill than the infection in his lungs and gaping wound.

Gently, he asked Bill if there was anyone whom he needed to forgive. "Oh, yeah," Bill responded. "Plenty. But the person I hate is my old lady. She ran out on me."

My friend reminded Bill of his weakened physical condition, the unlikely prospect of being able to get the surgery he needed, and the real possibility of death. "Would you like to pray to forgive your ex-wife?" my friend asked.

"I don't have anything to lose, do I, Doc?" Bill replied.

As they joined together in prayer, Bill cried and sobbed. Deep tears broke through the hardness of his heart, which had imprisoned him. Liberating tears flowed, which freed him from the chains of unforgiveness. Healing tears soothed the infected areas of his soul with the sweet balm of God's mercy. "Doc," Bill said, "I haven't felt this good in years. Thank you for praying with me."

The next day, when Bill's X rays were read, the radiologist was astonished by what they showed. The virulent infection that had been slowly poisoning him to death was completely gone. His lungs were spotless and clear. And there was no medical explanation for it. Bill had been miraculously healed through the act of forgiveness.

Surgery was done. The wound on his back closed. Bill eventually left the hospital to resume a new life transformed by the mercy of God active within him. As marvelous as Bill's physical healing was, it did not compare to the healing that had taken place in his heart. His cooperation with God's grace of forgiveness had healed him, body and soul. He was a new man in Christ Jesus.

The Healing Waters of God's Love

Yet another story points out how healing is released in us when we forgive. Audrey's home life as a child had been terrible. She was born to teenage parents whose immaturity had deeply scarred her. Their irresponsibility produced a sense of abandonment within Audrey which anchored in her heart and clung to her spirit even though she was now married and had children of her own.

Audrey came to the healing service aware that God had been working within her. Not long ago, she had surrendered to Him her profound sense of loneliness and neglect. In prayer, God had shown her how He had always been with her even in the most difficult of her childhood experiences.

But God had revealed even more to her in prayer. He had allowed a buried memory to surface in Audrey's consciousness that would be a key to her continued healing. She remembered that when she was three years old, she almost drowned in a local lake.

Audrey recalled that her parents had left her on the beach with a family friend. She remembered that she missed her parents and thought if she could only cross the lake she would find them. And so, she waded into the water. The woman, preoccupied with her own child, didn't notice.

At first all was fine because the water was shallow. But, as Audrey drifted further and further from shore, the sandy ledge suddenly dropped off and she began to sink into the lake's watery silence. With crystal clarity Audrey remembered choking and struggling for air. She remembered the engulfing darkness that crept over her like the stillness of night. She remembered giving in to it; and then, she remembered no more. For thirty years, this memory had been shrouded in secrecy. Audrey's parents had never mentioned it to her in all of her growing up years.

However, the Lord continued to bring more and more about the day's events into the light. Through the "chance" telephone call of an old family friend, Audrey discovered that her memory was true. The family friend even knew the person who had rescued Audrey—it was the woman who had been watching her on the beach. Audrey decided to contact her.

The telephone rang and the woman answered. Audrey told her who she was and thanked her for saving her life. The woman told Audrey she was more than welcome. And then, Audrey asked her the question that was troubling her: How did her parents react?

Tenderly, the woman told her that Audrey's parents were angry with Audrey for the disruption she had caused. With indifference and lack of concern they walked away as she sat in her rescuer's lap, choking and vomiting water. Her rescuer was shocked and worried for the little one she held close to her.

As Audrey listened to these words in stunned silence, another memory came out of the shadows; she recalled how she felt as her parents walked away—the awful stabbing certainty that they didn't love her. It was in that traumatic moment that abandonment had gripped her heart, a feeling that had held her captive all these years.

God had brought Audrey to the healing service to continue the healing process He had begun in her. He wanted Audrey to see herself as His daughter whom He had chosen in love from all eternity to have life. And He wanted to set her free from the shackles of abandonment that imprisoned her heart.

The healing service began with an exhortation to forgive. The speaker shared a story about a crippled woman who regained the use of her legs when she forgave her mother for the hurt she had caused her. Audrey listened to this story in awe. She knew that God was asking her to forgive her mother, and yet, the pain was too intense.

As the healing service progressed, the Lord continued to minister to Audrey. He began to reveal through words of knowledge[5] how He was healing His people and setting them free. One of the words said the Lord wanted to heal those who had painful memories associated with bodies of water. Audrey recounted, "The mention of swimming in the lake struck at my center to a wound not yet healed.... I knew the Lord wanted to dig it out at its core." Audrey knew the core of her problem was unforgiveness.

As the speaker led the participants in a prayerful meditation about forgiveness, tears welled up in Audrey's eyes. They spilled over and ran down her cheeks—washing away the heartache of abandonment, releasing the loneliness which clung to her heart, setting her free from years of pain.

Audrey's tears were a sign of the living water that was flooding her soul. God was pouring His healing love into her heart. She could feel it penetrating deeply into her being—renewing her, rejuvenating her, invigorating her.

In the inner confines of her heart, she heard God say, "You have a choice; you can choose rejection or you can choose love. You can continue to choke or you can allow Me to fill you with My breath—the breath of My love." In that moment, Audrey chose love. She forgave her parents and extended to them what she had received—the love and mercy of God. Audrey was healed.

There is one addendum to this story. Throughout her life, Audrey suffered from chronic asthma and sinus problems. Her nights were filled with fits of coughing and choking that disturbed her sleep. After the healing service, Audrey's bouts with choking and coughing stopped. No longer was she held captive by a hidden memory—in body or spirit.

Arise From the Darkness

St. Paul cries out to the Philippians, "I want to know [Christ] and the power of his resurrection ... if somehow I may attain the resurrection from the dead" (Phil 3:10-11, NAB). The Risen Jesus wants to meet us in the tomblike places within our hearts:

Those places that have been made cold and barren by the sins committed against us.

Those places shrouded in darkness and fear.

Those places where sin has carved wounds and injury into the delicate fiber of our being.

Those places where unforgiveness chains us to stony hostility.

Jesus comes with resurrection power to release us and set us free—to restore us, to renew us, to revitalize us, and to raise us from the dead. Sometimes our inner healing happens in the twinkling of an eye. Frequently, it takes days, months, or years. Occasionally, it takes a lifetime. But, in all cases, when we surrender to the action of God within us, healing comes. Freedom comes. Resurrection comes.

God is asking us to submit to His healing love that we might be a source of strength and healing for others. In the image of the Sacred Heart, Jesus points to the radiant splendor of His heart on fire with love for us. Into that all-consuming blaze we must place our doubts, our fears, our insecurities. We must place into that holy heart all of those areas of our lives that need to experience wholeness and health, all of those painful memories that have wounded our soul, all of those encumbrances of spirit that hold us back from fully surrendering to the love of God.

Then, even as we are being healed, we will be ready to fulfill our holy mission to aid humanity in not falling and to be the healers of the world. Then, and only then, will we discover that our own suffering is the source of consolation for the sufferings of others (see 2 Cor 1:3–7).

Carrying Out the Mission: Embracing the Abundant Life

We need heralds of the Gospel who are experts in humanity, who know the depths of the heart of many today, who share in his hopes and joys, his worries and his sadness, and at the same time are contemplatives, in love with God. For this, new saints are needed. The great evangelizers ... have been saints. We must implore God to increase the spirit of holiness in the Church and to send us new saints to evangelize today's world.

POPE JOHN PAUL II,
ADDRESS TO EUROPEAN BISHOPS
OCTOBER 11, 1985

With these words Pope John Paul II reminds us that, in every day and age, God chooses individuals to bear the image of His Son to the world. In this our day and age, you and I have been chosen for this holy mission. Everything about us is ordered for its completion. Our gifts and talents, our personality traits and temperament, our energies and inclinations, even the timing of our birth—all of these have been ordained by God so that we might be a vessel of His love in the world today.

But it is the gift of our gender, with its life-bearing capacity, which makes us as women particularly well-suited to fulfill this mission in our day and time. When we accept our call to spiritual motherhood, a call that is rooted in our feminine nature, we become a healing balm, a nurturing influence, a sustaining force which enables the human person to live out the fullness of life that God intends for him. As we receive the grace of authentic femininity through conformity to God's will, our hearts are impregnated with the seed of charity. Like our physical wombs, which expand with the development of our children, the wombs of our hearts grow large as love and mercy develop within us—so large do they grow that the joys and hopes, the pains and frustrations, the worries and sadness of mankind can be carried within them.

Because God has created woman to be life-bearer both physically and spiritually, it is in loving and giving that we women discover the profound dignity of our position in the kingdom of God. We discover that just as God entrusted His Son to the ministry of a woman, so too He has entrusted the whole of mankind to woman's ministry. And from this knowledge and our acceptance of it, we grow in strength and confidence. "A woman is strong because of her awareness of this entrusting, strong because of the fact that God 'entrusts the human being to her,' always and in every way, even in the situations of social discrimination in which she finds herself."[1]

That is why the Fathers of the Second Vatican Council entrust to her the future of the human race:

> *You women have always had as your lot the protection of the home, the love of beginnings, and an understanding of cradles. You are present in the mystery of a life beginning. You offer consolation in the departure of death. Our technology runs the risk of becoming*

inhuman. Reconcile men with life and above all, we beseech you, watch carefully over the future of our race. Hold back the hand of man who, in a moment of folly, might attempt to destroy human civilization.[2]

Woman, fully surrendered to the grace of her gender, is called to be a redeeming and sanctifying influence in the world. An influence that preserves and protects the physical and spiritual well-being of the human race.

Our previous chapters have discussed how we become vessels of God's love by cooperating with the grace He gives us to grow in holiness. In this final chapter we will explore how we can share God's love with others and thus fulfill our mission of spiritual motherhood. Mary, our spiritual Mother, is the one who will show us the way as we seek to be Christ-bearers.

Mary, Our Spiritual Mother

Early Church history shows that the Blessed Virgin Mary played a unique role in the life of the early Christians. This role is seen in the prayer that is considered to be the most ancient of all prayers to her, dating all the way back to the third century. It is called the *Sub Tuum:*

We fly to your protection, O Holy Mother of God, despise not our necessities, but deliver us from all danger, ever glorious and blessed Virgin.

While this prayer tells us much about what the early Christians knew about the Blessed Mother—that she was *Theotokos,* "God-Bearer," and that she was ever-virgin—it also tells us that they prayed to her in their need and regarded her prayers as efficacious. Thus, since the earliest days of Church history, Mary, our Mother, has been regarded as one who mediates for the people of God.

A mediator serves as a vehicle for bringing about reconciliation and unity between two or more parties. Jesus Christ is the one mediator between God and man (see 1 Tm 2:5-6). But, by virtue of our Baptism, which makes us coheirs with Jesus Christ, each of us is called to participate and share in His mediation to the Father. As the Second Vatican Council states: "No creature could ever be counted along with the Incarnate Word and Redeemer; but just as the priesthood of Christ is shared in various ways both by his ministers and the faithful, and as the one goodness of God is radiated in different ways among his creatures, so also the unique mediation of the Redeemer does not exclude but rather gives rise to a manifold cooperation which is but a sharing in this one source."[3]

These words from Vatican II echo the teaching of St. Thomas Aquinas: "Christ alone is the perfect mediator between God and man ... but there is nothing to prevent others in a certain way from being called mediators between God and man in so far as they, by preparing or serving, cooperate in uniting men to God."[4] These others who prepare, serve, and cooperate in uniting men to God are called secondary mediators.

Scripture is filled with examples of secondary mediators. In the Old Testament, Moses and Abraham are examples of individuals who acted as mediators between God and man. The prophets, such as Ezekiel and Jeremiah, also functioned as instruments of unity. Angels such as Gabriel and Raphael were used by God in profound ways as messengers of His will.

In New Testament times, following the Ascension of Jesus, we also see illustrations of secondary mediation. The miraculous healings that took place through the intercession of the disciples, the proclamation of the faith through the apostles, and the celebration of the Eucharistic meal all provide a clear example of how the baptized are called to share in the priestly role of Christ as mediator.

A Closer Look at Mary's Role

But how is it that the early Christians saw Mary in this role as a mediator? Mary's mediation flows directly from her position as the Mother of Jesus Christ and, therefore, the Mother of the Mystical Body. According to St. Paul, Christ is the Head of the body and the Church is the body of Christ. Because Mary conceived Jesus Christ who is the Head of the body, she also conceived all of the faithful, since, through Baptism, we are members of this same body. When Mary gave birth to Jesus, she made it possible for all of us to receive spiritual life through Him. Thus, she is our spiritual Mother.[5]

Pope Pius X beautifully stated this concept. He said, "Mary, bearing in her own womb the Savior, may be said to have borne also those whose life was contained in the life of the Savior. All of us, therefore … have come forth from the womb of Mary as a body united to its head. Hence, in a spiritual and mystical sense, we are called children of Mary, and she is the Mother of us all."[6]

Jesus Himself was the One who gave His Mother to the faithful members of His body. In His moment of agony, He looked down from the cross at John, the beloved disciple, and said to His Mother, "Woman, behold your son." And to John, "There is your Mother." In so doing, He gave His Mother to the whole human family, represented in the person of John. The gospel passage tells us that from this moment forward John welcomed Mary, the Mother of Christ, into his home.

In the biblical understanding, to welcome someone into one's home is to welcome someone into one's heart. We are all called to be "beloved disciples." Jesus' action of giving His Mother to St. John indicates that He is giving her to each of us. In like fashion, St. John's action of receiving Mary as His Mother exemplifies what our action toward her should be.

However, Mary's function as our spiritual Mother in no way depends upon our acknowledging the fact. Her role in salvation history was determined by God the Father and is fulfilled through her obedience to Him. She remains the spiritual Mother of the faithful whether the faithful accept her in this role or not.

Through her role as spiritual Mother, the Blessed Virgin Mary functions as mediator in many ways. We will look at three of these ways and see how these methods of mediation indicate how we, as women in the world today, are called to be mediators—individuals who seek to work with the Redeemer in bringing mankind to God. In imitating our Mother through these methods of mediation we will carry out our mission to aid humanity in not falling and to be the healers of the world.

The Blessed Virgin Mary mediates in these three ways:

- Mary mediates by bringing the Word of God to the world;
- Mary mediates through intercession;
- Mary mediates by sharing in the sufferings of her Son.

Mary Brings the Word of God to the World

Because of her "yes" to God at the moment of her Annunciation, Mary is intimately involved in the task of redemption. We read in Galatians 4:4, "But when the time had fully come, God sent forth his Son, *born of woman*." Though Mary is but a creature like you and me, through her womb and from her genes came the One who is Redeemer. Mary's "yes" literally gave flesh to God's plan for salvation. In this way, Mary mediated by being a channel for

God's redemptive grace to enter the world. She literally brought the Word of God to the world.

Like Mary, our spiritual Mother, we are called to be mediators by bringing the Word of God to others. Though the Blessed Virgin Mary is the only person to bring Jesus Christ into the world physically, by virtue of our Baptism each of us is called to bring God's word to others by proclaiming the Good News of salvation. The Documents of the Second Vatican Council tell us that, as laity, we have an assignment in the mission of the whole people of God; namely, to work at the evangelization and sanctification of mankind. Pope John Paul II reminds us that "every Christian has to participate in the task of Christian formation, to feel the urgent need to evangelize—something, says St. Paul, 'that gives me no ground for boasting. For necessity is laid upon me.'"[7]

Like Mother, Like Daughter: Called to Be Mediators

You and I together have been called to be ambassadors of Christ Jesus in the world (see 2 Cor 5:20). And what could be a more glorious call than to proclaim the marvelous truth of our salvation?

Why, then, do we resist this call? Three excuses head the list when it comes to finding reasons not to share our faith:

- "It's not my job!"
- "I don't know enough."
- "I don't want to offend anyone."
  Let's take a look at each of these.

"It's Not My Job!"

We have already seen through Scripture and the teachings of the Roman Catholic Church that evangelization is a mission for each baptized person. And since God commissions us to do it, we know

He has given us the grace through our Baptism to accomplish it. St. Gregory the Great tells us, "Each one should examine themselves to see how energetically they are working in the vineyard of the divine Sower. Perhaps we have not dedicated everything we have to the service of the Lord. The people who really work for him ... are those who are anxious to win souls and bring others to the vineyard."[8] *Excuse #1, then, doesn't excuse us.*

"I Don't Know Enough."

Many of us feel deficient when it comes to knowing Scripture by passage and verse. Still others of us wonder if we can present the truths of our faith in a clear and concise manner. These concerns may be valid. All of us fear that one question for which we have no answer. And perhaps this concern is precisely the incentive we need to dust off our Bibles and catechisms and begin to study our faith with greater fervor and diligence.

However, lack of knowledge does not excuse us from sharing our faith. Even if we do not have Scripture passages memorized, even if we do not feel as knowledgeable about our Faith as we'd like, each of us *does* know about our own experience with Jesus Christ. A most effective way to evangelize is simply to share our story. The *Catechism of the Catholic Church* puts it this way:

> The baptized have become "living stones" to be "built into a spiritual house, to be a holy priesthood" (1 Peter 2:5). By Baptism they share in the priesthood of Christ, in his prophetic and royal mission. They are "a chosen race, a royal priesthood, a holy nation, God's own people that [they] may declare the wonderful deeds of him who called [them] out of darkness into his marvelous light" (1 Peter 2:9).

CATECHISM, #1268

Sharing our own personal stories of God's action in our lives simply means we tell others about what God has done for us—*His wonderful deeds*—and how He called us out of the darkness of ignorance and sin and into *His marvelous light* of grace and knowledge.

In a television program we produced on evangelization, our guest shared with us an easy and efficient way to share our story. He suggested that we divide it into three parts: *I Was, He Did, I Am*. First, we tell others about the way we were before we entered into relationship with Jesus or called on Him for help. Then, we share with them about the moment of conversion that occurred in our lives, or a moment of grace that helped us in the midst of a struggle. Finally we outline the ways in which we have been touched, changed, healed by knowing Jesus in a personal way and being open to the grace He longs to give us. Sharing our personal stories is effective evangelization. It is nonthreatening, irrefutable, and engaging. It is one way we can all share our love of God.

"I Don't Want to Offend Anyone."

We can all relate to this excuse. Many of us have had the experience of being buttonholed on the street corner or opening our front door to find a person with the tenacity of a terrier waving tracts in our face. None of us wants to appear fanatical or pesky. How, then, do we sincerely share our faith without being offensive? I believe the answer to this question can be summed up in one word—*invitation*. We don't *impose,* we *propose.* Asking friends, coworkers, or family members to attend church with us or join us at a prayer meeting is often the invitation they have been waiting for. Many individuals have been led to Jesus after being invited to attend a Scripture study or discussion group about Christian living. All we need do is ask. The rest is up to the Holy Spirit.

Another effective way we can invite is by offering to pray with someone who shares his struggle with us. I always look at these opportunities as moments of grace. When those friends, co-workers, family members, or even strangers share their troubles with us, we can simply ask them, *"Would you mind if I said a prayer with you now?"* or, *"How about if we pray together about this?"* In all of the times I have asked this question—to the faithful and the faithless—I have rarely been refused. On the contrary, it has often opened the door for me to share my story with them.

Occasionally, however, we may be challenged on the truths of the faith or the Word of God. When this happens, charity must prevail. We must speak truth, but always with Christian love and fraternity. An angry, harsh word or an argumentative disposition is sure to plant hostility and misunderstanding rather than a seed of faith which may blossom later. Practicing patience, fortitude, and prudence in these moments is the mark of a true disciple.

I know of one person, for example, who invites every door-to-door evangelizer into his home. As they present their case, he patiently takes them through Scripture point by point, sharing with them the Truth who is Jesus Christ. Many members of false spiritualities and cults have come to the Lord because of his loving and charitable explanations.

The bottom line is that there is no excuse for not evangelizing. However, there are many instances when speaking may not be the best method to use. This is often the situation with loved ones who are not open to a relationship with Jesus for one reason or another. Sometimes just the mention of His name is enough to cause an ugly scene. We want our conversation to be a source of grace for those we wish to lead to Jesus, not a temptation for them to sin. In these cases, the way to evangelize is through intercessory prayer and the witness of our lives.

First, we begin to pray fervently for them. Intercessory prayer prepares the field of the heart to receive the seed of truth. Truth cannot grow in a heart that has not been prepared. Till the soil of your loved one's heart with your steadfast and earnest prayer.

The next step is a difficult one. Wait. Wait until you know the soil of the heart has been made ready. You will know the time is right when the opportunity to evangelize comes through the person you have been praying for. He or she may ask you a question or come to you for advice. They may share a trial with you or express their concern over a situation in their lives. This is your cue that the time is right. Ask them if they would like to pray about their struggle or if they would like to hear your story. Let your loved one lead the conversation; if they pursue, continue; if they are quiet, then you be quiet. With such a caring exchange, the seed of truth can gently begin to take root in his or her heart.

Finally, once you speak the truth, water that seed with continued prayer, love, support, even fasting. Sometimes you will see rapid changes. Sometimes the change will be imperceptible. Sometimes there will be no change. Do not lose heart. Remember, St. Monica prayed for St. Augustine for many years. Time is not important, only eternity. A passage from St. James speaks to this situation beautifully: "Be patient, therefore, brethren, until the coming of the Lord. Behold, the farmer waits for the precious fruit of the earth, being patient over it until it receives the early and the late rain. You also be patient. Establish your hearts, for the coming of the Lord is at hand" (Jas 5:7-8).

Along with intercessory prayer, the daily witness of our lives is the most effective means of evangelizing those we love. Our actions and reactions, our words and attitudes, constantly speak of our own relationship with God. In our homes, offices, and places of recreation we must recognize that God has asked us to be "the salt of the earth ... the light of the world" (Mt 5:13-14). Jesus tells us that our light must shine before men, "that they may see your good works and give glory to your Father who is in heaven" (Mt

5:16). Our everyday relationships with family, friends, coworkers, and neighbors provide tangible evidence of our personal conversion and transformation. Therefore, we must always hunger for our own ongoing evangelization by asking God to purify us and make us holy. Through intercessory prayer and the daily witness of our lives, those we care about are sure to come to the Lord. Remember, "The prayer of a righteous man has great power in its effects" (Jas 5:16).

Each day God gives us countless opportunities to share the healing love of Jesus Christ with others. We must pray for the spiritual vision to see these opportunities and the grace to act upon them in truth and in love. "On all Christians, accordingly, rests the noble obligation of working to bring all men throughout the world to hear and accept the divine message of salvation."[9]

Like Mary, our spiritual Mother, you and I as women have been chosen by God in a particular way to bear Christ to the world. May we accept this mission with confidence, assurance, and purpose—as women anointed and sent by God. Thus we will follow in the example of our Mother to be a mediator in today's world.

Mary Intercedes for God's Children

The mediation of the Blessed Virgin Mary includes not only bringing the Word of God to the world but also in bringing the world to the Word of God. Pope John Paul II says that "Mary, the exalted Daughter of Sion, helps all her children, wherever they may be and whatever their condition, to find in Christ the path to the Father's house."[10]

The Blessed Virgin fulfills this maternal function of mediation by being an intercessor for her spiritual children. Just as a natural mother pleads for the welfare of her little ones, so too does the

Blessed Virgin Mary plead for the needs of her spiritual children before the throne of God. Thus, she "is invoked in the Church under the titles of Advocate, Helper, Benefactress, and Mediatrix."[11] Mary's role as mediator in this way does not diminish Jesus' position as the One Mediator between God and man, but rather, it "flows forth from the superabundance of the merits of Christ, rests on his mediation, depends entirely on it and draws all its power from it."[12]

Mary's role as an advocate is prefigured in the Old Testament and demonstrated in the New Testament. In the Old Testament, the kings of the Davidic line had numerous wives. As a result, it was the king's mother who was chosen to be the queen. As queen, she had various functions. She represented the needs of the people before the king, counseled the king regarding issues of the kingdom, and ruled the kingdom in the king's absence. Because of her family relationship to the king, the queen mother was a powerful and respected figure whose place at the king's right side denoted her honored position (see 1 Kgs 2:19-20; 2 Kgs 11:3; 1 Kgs 15:9-13).

Mary of Nazareth is the Mother of Jesus Christ, the King of Kings. As such, she is the great Queen Mother who sits at the right side of her Son in His heavenly kingdom. But even on earth she fulfilled her position as Queen Mother.

The wedding feast of Cana provides us with a good example (see Jn 2:1-10). Here, Mary functioned both as a counselor to the King and as an advocate of the people's needs. "They have no wine," she apprised her Son; and to the servants, knowing that her intercession would have the desired results, she said, "Do whatever he tells you." Thus, Mary both counseled her Son about an existing issue and then interceded ("advocated") for the needs of the people.

Still another example from the New Testament may well

provide us with an illustration of Mary fulfilling the role of Queen Mother. In this case, she may have been ruling the kingdom in the absence of the King. This scene takes place just prior to Pentecost. Jesus had ascended to heaven, and the frightened members of His kingdom on earth were clustered together in the Upper Room, waiting for the promised Paraclete. Scripture tells us that Mary, the Mother of Jesus, was there (see Acts 1:14).

Could it have been Mary in the role of Queen Mother who kept this quivering band together, reminding them of her Son's words, encouraging them to have faith, nurturing them as only a mother can? The Fathers of the Second Vatican Council tell us that Mary is the Mother of the Church (*Lumen Gentium,* #53). In a mystical sense, could it be that Mary, as Queen Mother, was ruling the infant Church while awaiting the descent of the Holy Spirit? While Scripture does not explicitly tell us this is the case, such actions would have been fully within the role of queen mother, and would have made perfect sense.

But it is in the Book of Revelation that we come to see the full measure of Mary as Queen Mother and advocate. "And a great portent appeared in heaven, a woman clothed with the sun, with the moon under her feet, and on her head a crown of twelve stars" (Rv 12:1). Mark Miravalle, S.T.D., theologian and Mariologist, writes:

> *Mary is the only Woman who will bring forth Christ the King, "who is to rule all nations with an iron rod" (Rev. 12:5). She is the Woman foreshadowed in Genesis who will battle the dragon-serpent in her mission with the Savior Son (cf. Gen. 3:15, Rev. 12:3-7). As the child (cf. Rev. 12:5) refers to the person of Jesus, so too, the woman who brought forth a child (cf. Rev. 12:5) refers to the person of Mary.... Mary, Queen Mother and Advocate, is crowned with the twelve stars (cf. Rev. 12:1), which symbolize both*

the twelve tribes of Israel and the twelve apostles of the new king-dom.... At the end of her earthly life and following her glorious Assumption into heaven, the Daughter of Zion is crowned as Queen in the Kingdom of God, in virtue of her participation in the conquest of the kingdom with the Redeeming Savior at the foot of the Cross (cf. John 19:26).[13]

Mary, the counselor and intercessor at Cana, the Queen Mother in the Upper Room, the Woman Clothed With the Sun, the Great Woman of Revelation, the Woman Assumed into Heaven, is the advocate for the people of God. *Lumen Gentium* says that "by her maternal charity, she cares for the brethren of her Son, who still journey on earth surrounded by dangers and difficulties, until they are led into their blessed home."

The same section of *Lumen Gentium* also tells us that Mary's intercession for the people of God "continues uninterruptedly from the consent which she loyally gave at the Annunciation and which she sustained without wavering beneath the cross, until the eternal fulfillment of all the elect. Taken up to heaven she did not lay aside this saving office but by her manifold intercession continues to bring us the gifts of eternal salvation."[14] Mary's intercession for her spiritual children will not stop until each of them receives the gift of salvation. She will advocate for them until the end of time.

Like Mother, Like Daughter: Called to Be Intercessors

Just as Mary, our Spiritual Mother, intercedes for each one of us before the throne of God, we, too, are to intercede for the needs of the world. Sometimes our intercession will be for a specific intention or individual, a family member or friend. Perhaps at other times it will be for a personal need we are experiencing—a disability or an illness, difficulties with our spouse or children, financial troubles, problems at work. At still other times, our intercession will be for the broader community in which we live—our neighborhood or school district; our city or state; our nation; an end to abortion, euthanasia, and infanticide; shelter for the homeless. Whatever the need or intention, when we stand before the throne of God, like our Mother, we will do much to aid humanity in not falling and to be the healers of the world.

Effective Intercessory Prayer

The dictionary defines *intercede* as "to mediate; to plead on behalf of another; to be an instrument of reconciliation between parties." As women who carry the needs of the world within the wombs of our hearts, we are called to be intercessors. Mary, our Spiritual Mother, shows us the five key actions that define the effective intercessor.

The effective intercessor is one who accepts the mission. It was because of Mary's "yes" to God that salvation entered the world and each of us was given the privilege of redemptive grace. If we are to be mediators of redemptive grace in our world today, we, too, must say "yes" to the call.

In Ezekiel 22 God lists for the prophet the many crimes of Jerusalem: sexual promiscuity, usury, a disregard for the dignity of the human person, godlessness, and murder. But then God says something to Ezekiel that should set us on the edge of our seats:

> *And I sought for a man among them who should build up the wall and stand in the breach before me for the land, that I should not destroy it; but I found none. Therefore I have poured out my indignation upon them; I have consumed them with the*

fire of my wrath; their way I have requited upon their heads, says the Lord God.

EZEKIEL 22:30-31

Here, God is sharing a deep spiritual truth with Ezekiel. He is saying that even though He sees the lack of morality in a nation, even though He sees man's inhumanity to man, even though a country may be godless, even though bloodshed may characterize a culture, if there is someone who is standing in the gap, who is making intercession, who is pleading before Him to save that people, that culture, that nation, then His wrath can be held back.

If this is the case over situations so devastating and sinful, then surely this same God of mercy will show kindness and love to the many petitions we bring to Him. Only one thing is required—individuals who are willing to accept the mission. God is looking for people today to stand in the gap and make intercession for the needs of the world. Are we willing to say "yes" as did Mary, our Spiritual Mother? Will we accept the mission?

The effective intercessor is one who perseveres in the call. The Fathers of the Second Vatican Council tell us that Mary will mediate for the people of God *"until the eternal fulfillment of all the elect."* This means that Mary *continues* to intercede for her spiritual children. We can take great comfort that, even as we read these words, Mary is before the Father's throne, commending to Him our needs and petitions.

If we are to be effective intercessors, in imitation of our Mother, we too must persevere—in season and out of season, when it is convenient and when it is not, when we feel like it and when we don't. Our commitment to the call must be foremost in our hearts and minds.

The Old Testament provides us with wonderful examples of

intercessors who persevere. One of my favorite intercessions is found in Genesis 18. Here, we see Abraham interceding on behalf of Sodom. The immorality of this city was legendary and God was intent on destroying it. But Abraham began to intercede on behalf of any innocent people who may have been living in Sodom. He asked God if He would spare the city if there were fifty innocent people in it. God said that if fifty people could be found, He would spare the city.

But fearing that fifty people could not be found, Abraham then pleaded with God to spare the city if forty-five could be found. Again, God agreed. However, Abraham feared that even forty-five could not be found, so he asked God to spare it if only forty could be found. And then if thirty could be found. And then, twenty. And finally, Abraham asked if God would spare the city if ten good people could be found. God assured Abraham that He would spare the city for the sake of the ten.

Though God ultimately destroyed Sodom because not even ten good people could be found, we discover much about His love, mercy, and justice from this story. We also discover much about the perseverance of an effective intercessor. Abraham was willing to beseech God. He was willing to advocate on behalf of those whom he believed to be innocent. He was willing to remain firm and persevere in spite of the fact that the prospects were not good. Abraham was untiring in his appeal to save the city for the sake of a few.

God's interaction with Abraham assures us that He desires to hear our appeals. He reveals to us in this story that He is a God who seeks to treat His children with mercy and desires to be persuaded on behalf of them, even though His sense of justice may indicate otherwise. Through this interaction between God and Abraham, we see the love of the Father's heart, and because of this love, we should feel encouraged to come before Him with our petitions and the petitions of others. All we need do is persevere in our call to be an advocate for the needs of the world. St. Frances Cabrini advises: "We must pray without tiring, for the salvation of mankind does not depend on material success; nor on sciences that cloud the intellect. Neither does it depend on arms and human industries, but on Jesus alone."[15]

An effective intercessor is one who guards herself against personal sin. The Blessed Virgin Mary was called "Full of Grace" by the Angel Gabriel. This name tells us that Mary was preserved from the stain of original sin. Like all human creatures, Mary was in need of a Savior. But, because God needed a sanctified and holy vessel to bear His Son to the world, He intervened at the moment of her conception and applied to her the favor of redemption in anticipation of the grace Jesus merited on Calvary. God, who exists in eternity, is not limited by time or space. This principle is called "preservative redemption."

Because she has never been tainted by the stain of sin, Mary's prayers have always been particularly efficacious. Personal sin never set up a barrier between her and God. The wounds of her heart never distorted her motivation nor blinded her to the truth. Lust for the passions of the world never corrupted her sensibilities nor her ability to conform to God's will. Mary has always made perfect intercession for her spiritual children.

Unlike Mary, we have not been preserved from original sin. You and I, along with the rest of humanity, come into the world with original sin and the predilection to sin we inherited from our first parents, Adam and Eve. Our personal sin sets up a labyrinth of darkness through which our intercessory prayer must travel. On its way it is contaminated by willful wants and desires. The wounds of our heart color our perceptions. Purity of intention is shadowed by selfish motivations.

But though our intercession is hampered by so many obstacles, we need not lose heart. God gives us the means to guard ourselves against personal sin. In His providence and love for us, He has given us the sacramental structure of our Catholic Church. In each sacrament, we receive sanctifying grace, which is a *"permanent principle of supernatural life*, a stable disposition found in the very essence of the soul."[16]

In his encyclical letter *Redemptoris Mater* (*Mother of the Redeemer*), Pope John Paul II tells us, "The effect of this eternal gift, of this grace ... is like a *seed of holiness*, or a spring which rises in the soul as a gift from God himself, who through grace gives life and holiness to those who are chosen" (par. 8).

You and I have been chosen by God from all eternity to receive the eternal gift of sanctifying grace. As we make use of the sacraments—especially the Sacrament of Reconciliation—our personal sin is absolved and our prayers of intercession can do much to aid humanity in not falling. The psalmist David understood the relationship between holiness and effective intercession. In Psalm 51, he writes:

> *Create in me a clean heart, O God,*
> *and put a new and right spirit within me.*
> *Cast me not away from thy presence,*
> *and take not thy holy Spirit from me.*
> *Restore to me the joy of thy salvation,*
> *and uphold me with a willing spirit.*
> *Then I will teach transgressors thy ways,*
> *and sinners will return to thee....*
> *The sacrifice acceptable to God is a broken spirit;*
> *a broken and contrite heart, O God,*
> *thou wilt not despise.*

PSALM 51:10-15, 17

Each time we seek the grace of forgiveness through the Sacrament of Reconciliation, we are fortified and strengthened against temptation, the power of sin loses its hold on us, and we are set free to be the healers of the world. To be an effective advocate for the people of God, we must beg God to create in us a clean heart, a heart washed in the blood of the Lamb.

Effective intercessors practice humility through mortification. Mary's life was one of conscious mortification, a voluntary practice of self-denial that aids us to conform to the will of the Father. From her *fiat* at the Annunciation to her pain at Golgotha, Mary submitted herself to the will of God, that His work might be accomplished.

With what humility she accepted the contradictions that her state in life produced! In her ninth month of pregnancy she journeyed to Bethlehem on the back of a donkey, gave birth to the Son of God in the bed of animals, escaped to Egypt like a fugitive, gave up her Son to public life, and finally buried Him in a borrowed tomb. At every turn, Mary sacrificed the simple pleasures a woman expects in life for the sake of God's kingdom. And, because of her humility, her offering bore great fruit in the hearts of men.

Like our Mother, we too are called to develop a spirit of humility through self-denial. When we enter into voluntary mortification, our spiritual vision becomes clearer and more focused. God's will stands out with greater clarity against the backdrop of our everyday circumstances. Coupling our prayers of intercession with a humility achieved through mortification releases a spiritual dynamic which makes our mediation more effective.

In 2 Chronicles 7:14, God makes a promise to all of His people regarding intercession offered in a spirit of humility through mortification. God says, "If my people who are called by my name humble themselves, and pray and seek my face, and turn from their wicked ways, then I will hear from heaven, and will forgive their sin and heal their land." Let us take this word to heart. God is showing us the means to effective intercession.

The effective intercessor is one who desires the will of God. Perhaps the most outstanding characteristic of the Blessed Virgin Mary is her complete submission to the will of God. So submissive was she to the Father's will that her only concern was to see it accomplished fully and completely in her. "Be it done unto me according to your word," she said to the Angel Gabriel.

Praying in accordance with God's will is the hallmark of an effective intercessor. God presents His will to us in Sacred Scripture and through the teachings of the Roman Catholic Church. As we read and study the Bible, the documents of the Church, and the *Catechism of the Catholic Church,* we grow in our knowledge of God's will and how it corresponds to individual circumstances.

While being an advocate according to God's will always starts with prayer, it often leads to action. Advocates are charged to preserve and protect what is God-honoring in the circumstances of our daily lives and the situations we confront in our culture. As mediators, we must seek righteousness, truth, and love. We must be willing to be vocal about issues that denigrate the human person, contribute to immorality, muddy the teaching of the Church, or seek to destroy the Judeo-Christian ethic. Such a position will not always make us popular or well-liked, but such a position will make us honest before the throne of God. And from such integrity can come true liberation for the people of God.

The place to advocate for the will of God is within our families, around our dinner tables, in our discussions with spouses, children, and friends. We must advocate for God's will on our school boards, in elementary and high school classrooms, and on college campuses. We must advocate for God's will in voting booths and boardrooms and hospitals. Advocacy for the will of God will lead us to speak for the unborn, the elderly, the sick and forsaken. It will take us into "the wide and complex arena of politics, sociology and economics ... the spheres of culture, the sciences, the arts, international relations and the communication media" (*Evangelization in the Modern World*, par. 70). And, in so doing, we will bear the presence of Jesus Christ to the world. These words of Blessed Josemaría Escrivá describe the effect of an advocate who is united to the will of God:

> *Among those around you, apostolic soul, you are the stone fallen into the lake. With your word and example produce a first ripple ... and it will produce another ... and then another, and another ... each time wider.*
>
> *Now do you understand the greatness of your mission?*[17]

Indeed, the mission to which God is calling us is a great one. He is asking us to stand in the gap, to make humble intercession before His holy throne for the needs of others and for the needs of the world. As we accept this call, we will do much to "aid humanity in not falling" and to heal the brokenness of the world.

Mary Shares in the Sufferings of Her Son

There is yet a third way in which Mary, our Spiritual Mother, mediates on behalf of the children of God. This way is by sharing in the sufferings of her Son, Jesus Christ. As we have mentioned, when Mary consented to bring Jesus Christ, the Word of God, into the world, she became a unique participant in the plan of redemption. Mary gives birth to Jesus Christ, the God-man, the

"New Adam." As Mother of the Redeemer, Mary is the "New Eve," the new Mother of the living.

The Church has always recognized her singular participation in salvation history and has referred to her by many names to express her role. One of these names is co-redemptrix.[18] This name does not mean that Mary is *equal* to Jesus, or that she redeemed mankind *like* Jesus. Rather, it simply means that Mary gave herself fully to God's plan in bringing salvation to the world. Remember how necessary was her "yes" for Jesus to be born. Likewise, everyone who says "yes" to God and cooperates with Him to bring the redemptive grace of Jesus Christ to other is a co-redeemer, *working with the Redeemer* in the vineyard for the salvation of souls.

However, we know Mary's role in the work of redemption extended far beyond her initial consent. Her "yes" extended all the way to Calvary. In a unique way, Mary participated in the Passion and death of her Son, Jesus Christ. At Jesus' presentation, Simeon prophesied, "Behold, this child is destined for the fall and rise of many in Israel, and to be a sign that will be contradicted (and you yourself a sword will pierce) so that the thoughts of many hearts may be revealed" (Lk 2:34-35, NAB). One commentary notes this about Simeon's prophecy of Mary's suffering: "The words Simeon addresses to Mary announce that she will be intimately linked with her Son's redemptive work. The sword indicates that Mary will have a share in her Son's sufferings; hers will be an unspeakable pain which pierces her soul. Our Lord suffered on the cross for our sins, and it is those sins which forge the sword of Mary's pain."[19]

In *Salvifici Doloris,* Pope John Paul II says that "It was on Calvary that Mary's suffering, beside the suffering Jesus, reached an intensity which can hardly be imagined from a human point of view, but which was mysteriously and supernaturally fruitful for the Redemption of the world. Her ascent of Calvary and her standing at the foot of the cross … were a special sort of sharing in the redeeming death of her Son" (par. 25).

The Blessed Virgin Mary gave herself totally to God, uniting all of her sufferings, all of her travails, all of her life's situations, culminating in that horrific moment on Calvary's hill, to the redemptive work of her Son. Her action was one of total donation. This gift of self was not marked by passivity nor resignation. Rather, it was a free-will offering of body, mind, and spirit, springing from a heart permeated with love, a heart whose sole desire was to give all of itself to its Beloved.

Mary embraced all that God gave her in love, peace, and joy.

Thus, in a wholly singular way she cooperated by her obedience, faith, hope and burning charity in the work of the Savior in restoring supernatural life to souls. For this reason she is mother to us in the order of grace. This motherhood of Mary in the order of grace continues uninterruptedly from the consent which she loyally gave at the Annunciation and which she sustained without wavering beneath the cross, until the eternal fulfillment of all the elect.[20]

Mary unites her own suffering to the suffering of her Son, Jesus Christ, and in so doing her suffering, like His, becomes a source of new life in the world. In this unique and salutary way, Mary works with the Redeemer in restoring supernatural life to souls.

Like Mother, Like Daughter: Called to Be Co-Redeemers

Because Mary is our Spiritual Mother, God's action in her prefigures His desired action in us, and Mary's response to God's initiative of grace exemplifies what our own response to God's movement in our lives should be. Therefore, Mary's complete and total act of self-donation signifies that we, too, are called by God to give ourselves to Him completely and without reservation. So too, we are to see all of life's difficulties and contradictions, struggles and pain, sufferings and travail, as opportunities to be united to Christ's saving action upon Calvary.

By embracing what comes our way with obedience, faith, hope, and burning charity, like our Mother, we will labor alongside of Christ in the work of salvation and thus be co-redeemers in the world today.

Throughout the history of the Church, the centrality of the cross and our union with it lie at the heart of the Christian experience. It is from the cross that we draw our faith, from the cross that we draw our hope, and from the cross that we draw our ability to love. The cross is the ultimate expression of God's power, for through it, Satan, sin, and death are conquered. Implicit, then, in the crucifixion of Christ is the wisdom of God. "For the word of the cross is folly to those who are perishing, but to us who are being saved it is the power of God" (1 Cor 1:18).

In Philippians 3:10-11, Paul tells us what we gain as we appropriate the grace of the cross to our own lives. He says, "I want to know Christ and the power of his resurrection and the sharing of his sufferings by becoming like him in his death, if somehow I may attain the resurrection from the dead" (NRSV).

If we want to experience resurrection power, our lives must be a participation in the Passion of Jesus Christ—a participation marked by total self-donation. We must strive, through the crosses which punctuate our lives, to share in the sufferings of Christ. When our daily sufferings are united to the cross of Christ with obedience, faith, and love, we will go forward in hope to the final resurrection.

Blessed Josemaría Escrivá exhorts us:

Here, before the cross, we should have sorrow for our sins and for those of all men…. And we should pray so that Christ's life and death may become the model and motivation for our own life and self-giving. Only thus will we earn the name of conquerors: for the risen Christ will conquer in us, and death will be changed into life.[21]

For Christians in every age, the message of salvation that comes to us through the cross of Christ and His resurrection gives us the ability to carry on in the midst of adversity, trial, and suffering. As Blessed Josemaría tells us, all that we have considered to be death comes to life and glows with the brilliance of fire-tried gold when united to the cross of Christ. For the saint, the cross itself, along with the suffering it entails, becomes the greatest of joys, for by suffering along with the crucified Jesus, we become a means of redemption in the world today.

Thus, St. Paul tells the Colossians, "Now I rejoice in my sufferings for your sake, and in my flesh I am filling up what is lacking in the afflictions of Christ on behalf of his body, which is the church" (Col 1:24, NAB). So, too, are we being called by God today to lay hold of the reality of the cross, its wisdom and its power, its efficacy and merit, that we might be inundated, saturated, filled to overflowing with the new life that comes through the Resurrection. A life that vivifies not only the innermost recesses of our souls, but a life that restores to life that which was dead in others.

Writing in *The Risen Christ*, Caryl Houselander, a contemporary mystic, tells us this about the meaning of Jesus' suffering, death, and resurrection and their relation to our suffering:

He, in his sacred humanity, could suffer no more; he could not be wounded or die any more; his life had become peace, joy, the absolute power of consummated love; and now by a supreme expression of that love, which completely passes our understanding and our realization, he gives us that life of joy. He gives that joy and peace to be at the very heart of our suffering, to make suffering and joy, for us as it was for him, not two things incompatible with each other, but just one thing, love—and he gives us his own power of consummated love to use for one another, to comfort and heal and restore one another; even, in a mysterious sense that those who have really known sin and sorrow and love will understand, to raise one another from the dead.[22]

St. Thérèse of Lisieux, the Little Flower, says that the way to heaven is paved for ourselves and for others through our sacrifices, great and small, united to the Passion of Christ. She writes:

I can truthfully say that, as soon as I entered Carmel, suffering stretched out her arms to me and I embraced her lovingly.... At the solemn examination before my Profession, I stated what I was going to do in Carmel: "I have come to save souls and, above all, to pray for priests." If one wants to achieve one's object, one has to use the right means, and as Jesus had told me He would give me souls through the Cross, I welcomed the Cross and my love of suffering grew steadily. For five years I trod this path, but no one else knew of it. This was the hidden flower I wanted to offer to Jesus, the flower which breathes its perfume only in the garden of heaven.[23]

And yet another time, she says:

Since our Well-Beloved has "trodden the wine press alone" (Is 63:3)—the wine which He gives us to drink—in our turn let us not refuse to wear garments dyed with blood, let us press out for Jesus a new wine which may slake His thirst, and looking around

Him He will no longer be able to say that He is alone; we shall be there to help (Is 63:5).[24]

Through uniting our sufferings, trials, and torments to the cross of Christ, we become co-redeemers with Him because we are there to help. Our "blood," intermingled with His, becomes a stream of redemptive life active in the world.

Uniting Our Sufferings to the Passion of Christ

How, then, do we practically go about uniting our sufferings to the cross of Christ to be used as a source of redemption for others? I believe St. Thérèse of Lisieux shows us the way in the excerpt from her autobiography.

First, while we do not look for suffering nor purposely bring it upon ourselves, when tribulation visits us, we embrace it.

This does not mean that we do not seek treatment for a health condition, nor does it mean that we do not seek ways to mitigate the trials we face in life. Nor does it mean that we stay in an abusive relationship or allow ourselves to be ill-treated. Rather, it means that for the duration of time in which we experience travail, we offer our suffering to God as a channel through which redemptive grace of Jesus Christ, can flow into the world.

We may choose to offer our suffering in reparation for our personal sin and for the sin of others. Or, we may choose to offer our suffering for a specific intention, for the poor souls in purgatory, for the needs of those we love, or for the work of a particular apostolate, missionary, or cause. In this way, we become a co-redeemer in the world. St. Thérèse demonstrates this valuable use of suffering when she says, "I have come to save souls and, above all, to pray for priests. If one wants to achieve one's object, one has to use the right means."

Second, we must look at suffering as a door through which grace walks into our souls and, in so doing, greet it with joy.
St. Thérèse tells us that she came to see that Jesus would win souls to Himself through her sufferings. Because of this realization her joy increased commensurately with the number of crosses she bore. To be sure, this is heroic virtue undergirded by a special grace from God. But it stands as an example for all of us, inviting us to accept every trial and tribulation with an eye toward the merit it can gain for the souls of others.

Joy is not a feeling of hilarity nor is it carefree abandon. Joy is not measurable by laughter, though laughter may express it. Rather, joy is a fruit of the Holy Spirit which rises from trust and surrender to the will of God. It is a peace and contentment which anchors the soul in true hope and faith. As our spiritual vision matures and we come to see the great benefit of uniting our sufferings to the Passion of Jesus, we begin to experience joy. It is through prayer that such insight comes. Prayer, in season and out, must be our constant companion if we are to fulfill our call to be co-redeemers.

Next, St. Thérèse tells us that she bore her sufferings in silence, and that her offering of pain to Jesus was known to Him alone.
Certainly the sisters in Thérèse's Carmel could see the debilitating effect of her illness. There was no question that they knew she was suffering. *Yet, she did not complain.* Thérèse did not assume the posture of a martyr, nor did she flaunt her suffering as a badge of courage. Rather, in meekness and humility she united her suffering to the cross of Christ that it might be used by Him as a conduit of grace. Thus, her silent witness not only was a means of grace for

the priests for whom she was offering her suffering, but it was also a means of great grace in the spiritual lives of the sisters within her convent. How many gained courage and strength through her? How many drew hope and faith from her? How many learned true charity of heart because of her?

Like the sacrificial offering of the Virgin Mary, St. Thérèse's act of self-donation laid bare the secret thoughts of many. In the midst of her suffering, borne with silent patience and love, she gently guided the souls of others to eternal salvation. We see this in the words she pens to her sister, Celine: "In our turn let us not refuse to wear garments dyed with blood ... and looking round Him He will no longer be able to say that He is alone; we shall be there to help."

Finally, Thérèse's letter gives us the greatest insight of all on how to fulfill our call to be a co-redeemer—we must prayerfully meditate on the Passion of Jesus Christ.

The rich imagery of St. Thérèse's words demonstrate her devotion to meditating on the Passion of Christ. Most of the great saints admitted that contemplation of the Passion yielded the choicest of fruit in their lives. Through prayerfully meditating on the sufferings of Christ, we arrive at a deeper understanding and appreciation for the gift of redemption and how we can cooperate with it. When we pray the Passion with thoughtful reflection, allowing God's great love for us to permeate our heart, the fire of holy zeal is ignited within and we desire to unite all of our sufferings to the cross of Christ, that they might be used by Him for the salvation of souls. Suffering becomes the sweetest of graces.

Through the vast treasure of devotion in the Holy Catholic Church we have no small number of ways to enter into praying the Passion. From the prayerful reading of the Gospel accounts to the Stations of the Cross to the Sorrowful Mysteries of the Rosary to contemplation before the crucifix to a holy study of sacred art, we have many ways of cultivating a deep love and reverence for the Passion of our Lord. All of these ways of prayer help us to nail our own difficulties and heartaches to Christ's cross for the redemption of the world.

When we embrace our sufferings with joy, accept them without complaint, and attach them to the sufferings of Christ, we imitate the Blessed Virgin Mary and are united to all of those holy people who lived out the call to be redeemers and sanctifiers of their day and age. And, in so doing, we do much to aid humanity in not falling.

The Hour Has Come: How Will We Respond?

"The hour is coming, in fact has come, when women imbued with the spirit of the Gospel will do much to aid humanity in not falling." This word, delivered in the Closing Speeches of the Second Vatican Council, was meant for you and me, and our response to it will shape the future of mankind.

As women empowered by the life of God active within us, we bring our spiritual motherhood to bear in all the aspects of our lives—in family life and professional life, in ministry and in social undertakings, into every arena of daily activity. To woman is entrusted the task and mission of passing on love and respect, understanding and compassion, hope and peace. To her is entrusted the task of nurturing the spiritual life of her children, bringing the reality of Christ to a broken world, being a symbol of truth and a sign of contradiction in a post-Christian age. Created in love, wholly for love, woman is meant to *be* love in the world. A love that spills over into words and deeds, relationships and inter-actions. A love that heals and restores, which chastens and makes new, which mends and reconciles. A love that transfigures and transforms.

Like the Blessed Virgin Mary, woman is called to receive the life of God within her through the power of the Holy Spirit, so that she becomes a channel through which love enters the world. A love truly able to aid humanity in not falling. Like our Mother we must bring God's word to His people, intercede before God's throne for the sake of the world, and unite our sufferings to the Passion and death of Jesus Christ. By so doing, we give birth to God's life in others and thus fulfill our divine mission of spiritual motherhood. This call is not for the fainthearted, but for women of courage, faith, perseverance, and hope:

> *The soul of a woman must ... be expansive*
> *and open to all human beings;*
> *It must be quiet,*
> *so that no small weak flame will be extinguished by stormy winds;*
> *warm,*
> *so as not to benumb fragile buds;*
> *clear,*
> *so that no vermin will settle in dark corners and recesses;*
> *self-contained,*
> *so that no invasions from without can peril the inner life;*
> *empty of itself,*
> *in order that extraneous life may have room in it;*
> *finally, mistress of itself, and also of its body,*
> *so that the entire person is readily at the disposal of every call.*[25]
>
> BLESSED EDITH STEIN

The whole of this book has been an attempt to form our souls according to this description of authentic femininity which Blessed

Edith Stein describes. We must be women who are spiritual mothers, women who are full of grace, women of the abundant life.

And so, the hour has come when God asks each one of us the only remaining question:

"My daughters, will you, like Mary your Mother, say 'yes' to your call and bring My life to the world?"

My dear sisters in Christ, the future of mankind depends on our answers.

NOTES

ONE
The Special Call and Gift of Woman

1. Vatican Council II, *Lumen Gentium*, par. 61. Unless otherwise stated, all references and citations from Vatican Council II are quoted from Austin Flannery, O.P., ed., *Documents of Vatican II, The Conciliar and Post Conciliar Documents*, rev. ed. (Northport, N.Y.: Costello, 1984).

2. Closing Speeches, Vatican Council II, *To Women*, read by Leon Cardinal Duval of Algiers, Algeria, assisted by Julius Cardinal Doepfner of Munich, Germany, and Raul Cardinal Silva of Santiago, Chile, December 8, 1965, printed by the Daughters of St. Paul, Boston, Mass., 29.

3. Louis Bouyer, *Woman in the Church*, trans. Marilyn Teichert (San Francisco: Ignatius, 1979), 62.

4. Robert C. Broderick, *The Catholic Encyclopedia* (Nashville: Nelson, 1976), 560.

5. Bouyer, 53.

6. Bouyer, 56. Emphasis added.

7. For a beautiful explanation of the word "munus," read the essay "The Importance of the Concept of 'Munus' to Understanding Humanae Vitae," written by Janet E. Smith and published in *Why Humanae Vitae Was Right: A Reader*, ed. Janet E. Smith (San Francisco: Ignatius, 1993), 307–24.

8. Edith Stein, "Ethos of Women's Professions," from *The Collected Works of Edith Stein*, vol. 2, *Essays on Woman*, trans. Freda Mary Oben (Washington, D.C.: ICS Publications, 1987), 43.

9. Closing Speeches, *To Women*, 29–30.

10. Joseph Cardinal Ratzinger, *Journey Towards Easter* (New York: Crossroad, 1987), 30. Emphasis added.

11. Pope John Paul II, *Mother of the Redeemer*, par. 46. Emphasis added.

12. Stein, 48–49.

13. Stein, 52.

14. Pope John Paul II, *On the Dignity and Vocation of Women*, par. 27.

15. Pope John Paul II, *Christifidelis Laici*, par. 16.

16. Stein, 51–52. Emphasis added.
17. Stein, 52. Emphasis added.

TWO
Prayer: Strength of the Abundant Life

1. St. Teresa of Avila, *The Life of Saint Teresa of Avila By Herself,* trans. J.M. Cohen (New York: Penguin, Classics ed., 1957), 63.
2. Louis Bouyer, *Introduction to Spirituality,* trans. Mary Perkins Ryan (Tournai: Desclee, 1961), 53.
3. Bouyer, *Introduction to Spirituality,* 54.
4. Vatican Council II, *Dei Verbum,* par. 21.
5. St. Francis de Sales, *Treatise of the Love of God,* bk. 6, ch. 3, quoted in Reginald Garrigou–Lagrange, O.P., *The Three Ages of the Interior Life,* vol. 2, trans. M. Timothea Doyle, O.P. (Rockford, Ill.: TAN, 1989), 280.
6. John A. Hardon, S.J., *The Question and Answer Catholic Catechism* (New York: Doubleday, 1981), 317.
7. Thomas Dubay, S.M., *Fire Within* (San Francisco: Ignatius, 1989), 57.
8. St. Francis de Sales, *Treatise,* bk. 6, ch. 7, from Garrigou-Lagrange, 281.
9. Dubay, 70.
10. An Irish Carmelite, *Thoughts of Saint Thérèse* (Rockford, Ill.: TAN, 1988), 127–28.
11. Bouyer, *Introduction to Spirituality,* 80.
12. Dubay, 70–71.
13. Franz Moschner, *Christian Prayer,* trans. Elisabeth Plettenberg (St. Louis: Herder, 1962), 187–88.
14. St. Teresa of Avila, *The Interior Castle,* trans. Kieran Kavanaugh, O.C.D. and Otilio Rodriguez, O.C.D. (New York: Paulist, 1979), Fourth Dwelling Place, ch. 1, no. 7, 70.

THREE
Praise and Petition, Thanksgiving and Contrition: Symphony of the Abundant Life

1. John Vianney, Sermon for the Fifth Sunday of Easter, quoted in Francis Fernandez, *In Conversation with God,* vol. 3, 40.1 (London: Scepter, 1992), 261.
2. St. Augustine, *Discourse of Psalm 148,* as referenced in *Liturgy of the Hours,* vol. 2 (New York: Catholic Book, 1976) 864–65.
3. St. Augustine, 864–65.
4. St. Augustine, 864–65.
5. St. Augustine, *The Confessions of St. Augustine,* (New York: New American Library, 1963), 235.
6. St. Catherine of Siena, *The Dialogue,* trans. Suzanne Noffke, O.P. (New York: Paulist, 1980), 365–66.
7. Merlin R. Carothers, *Power in Praise* (Escondido, Calif.: Merlin R. Carothers, 1972).
8. St. Augustine, *Commentary of Psalm 60, 2–3,* as referenced in *Liturgy of the Hours,* vol. 2, 87.
9. Amedee Brunot, S.C.J., *Mariam: The Little Arab,* trans. Jeanne Dumais, O.C.D.S., and Sister Miriam of Jesus, O.C.D. (Eugene, Ore.: The Carmel of Maria Regina, 1990), 180–81, quoted in Ronda De Sola Chervin, *Prayers of the Women Mystics* (Ann Arbor, Mich.: Servant, 1992), 180–81.

10. St. Augustine, *Letter 72*, quoted in Fernandez, vol. 5, 39.2, 222.
11. Franz M. Moschner, *Christian Prayer*, 35.
12. St. Francis de Sales, *Introduction to the Devout Life*, trans. and ed. by John K. Ryan (Garden City, N.Y.: Doubleday, Image Books, 1966) pt. 3, no. 5, 135.
13. St. Bernard, *Sermon for the Sixth Sunday after Pentecost*, 25, 4, quoted in Fernandez, vol. 5, 39.2, 224.
14. St. Thomas Aquinas, *Summa Theologica*, trans. Fathers of the English Dominican Province (Allen, Tex.: Christian Classics, 1981), vol. 3, pt. 2–2, q. 83, a. 2, 1533.
15. Josemaría Escrivá, *The Way* (Princeton, N.J.: Scepter, 1982), par. 101, 33.

FOUR
Obedience: Power for the Abundant Life

1. Pope John Paul II, *Christifideles Laici*, par. 17.
2. Raniero Cantalamessa, *Obedience* (Boston: St. Paul, 1989), 27.
3. Cantalamessa, 19, quoting St. Basil, Reg. Fus. Proem. PG 31, 896.
4. Cantalamessa, 23.
5. Cantalamessa, 23–24, Cantalamessa in part quoting Diadochus Phot, Cap. gnost. 4; S.Ch. 5, 86.
6. Adolphe Tanquerey, *The Spiritual Life*, trans. Herman Branderis (Tournai, Belgium: Desclee, 1930), par. 479, 233.
7. St. Francis de Sales, *Treatise of the Love of God*, quoted in bk. 8, c. 3 (Mackey's translation, 329) Tanquerey, par. 480. .
8. Pope John Paul II, *Tertio Millennio Adveniente*, par. 36.
9. Garrigou-Lagrange, vol. 1, 206–13.
10. Garrigou-Lagrange, 206–13.
11. Tanquerey, par. 482, 235.

FIVE
Wisdom: Vision for the Abundant Life

1. Fernandez, vol. 2, 89.1, 549.
2. Garrigou-Lagrange, vol. 2, 232.
3. Tanquerey, par. 479, 233.
4. Tanquerey, par. 486, 236.
5. St. Bernard, *I Serm. S. Adreae*, 5, quoted in Tanquerey, par. 492, 239.
6. Louis Colin, C.SS.R., *The Interior Life*, trans. by Sister Maria Constance, S.C.H. (Westminster, Md.: Newman, 1962), 146–47.
7. Fernandez, vol 2, 22.2, 135.
8. Tanquerey, par. 1020–25, 481–83.
9. Tanquerey, par. 1174, 553.
10. The Marian Servants of Divine Providence is a Private Association of the Christian Faithful located in the Diocese of St. Petersburg, Florida. To find out more about the Marian Servants, the ministries it operates, and the chapter nearest you, contact 1-800-558-5452.
11. Bouyer, *Introduction to Spirituality*, 283.
12. Thomas Dubay, *Seeking Spiritual Direction: How to Grow the Divine Life Within* (Ann Arbor, Mich.: Servant, 1993), 32.

13. Pope Leo XIII, *Testem Benvolentiae*, January 22, 1899, quoted by Tanquerey, par. 531, 257–58.
14. St. Francis de Sales, *Introduction to the Devout Life*, pt. 1, no. 4, 45.
15. St. John of the Cross, *Complete Works III, Spiritual Sentences and Maxims*, 219, quoted by Fernandez, vol. 5., 85.3, 492.
16. St. John Climacus, *Stairs of Paradise*, as quoted in Fernandez, vol. 1, 7.3, 53–54.
17. St. Teresa of Avila, *The Way of Perfection*, trans. E. Allison Peers (New York: Doubleday, Image Books, 1991), 259.
18. Dubay, *Seeking Spiritual Direction*, 55–62.
19. Garrigou-Lagrange, vol. 1, quoted by Fernandez, vol. 1, 7.3, 53–54.
20. St. Francis de Sales, *Introduction to the Devout Life*, pt. 1, ch. 4, 47.
21. St. Teresa of Avila, *Life*, 94.
22. St. John of the Cross, *The Living Flame of Love, The Collected Works*, st. 3, par. 30, 684–85.
23. Dubay, *Seeking Spiritual Direction*, 77–78.
24. Dubay, *Seeking Spiritual Direction*, 81.
25. Tanquerey, par. 551–55, 267–70.
26. St. Francis de Sales, *Introduction to the Devout Life*, pt. 1, ch. 4, 47.
27. St. Francis de Sales, *Introduction to the Devout Life*, pt. 1, ch. 4, 46–47.
28. Tanquerey, par. 556, 269.
29. Tanquerey, par. 557, 269–70.
30. Dubay, *Seeking Spiritual Direction*, 117–52.
31. Dubay, *Seeking Spiritual Direction*, 131.
32. Dubay, *Seeking Spiritual Direction*, 136.
33. Pope John Paul II, *Christifideles Laici*, par. 58.

SIX
Eucharist: Heart of the Abundant Life

1. Pope Paul, IV *Mysterium Fidei*, par. 69.
2. St. Ignatius of Antioch, *Letter to the Smyrnaeans (110 AD)*, quoted by William A. Jurgens, *The Faith of the Early Fathers* (Collegeville, Minn.: Liturgical, 1970), vol. 1, par. 64, 25.
3. St. Justin Martyr, *First Apology*, quoted by Jurgens, par. 128, 55.
4. St. Irenaeus, *Against Heresies*, quoted by Jurgens, par. 249, 99.
5. St. Athanasius, *Sermon to the Newly Baptized*, quoted by Jurgens, par. 802, 345.
6. St. Cyril of Jerusalem, 22 (*Mystagogic* 4), 4, quoted by Jurgens, par. 846, 361.
7. St. Augustine, *Sermons 227, 21*, quoted by Jurgens, vol. 3, par. 1519, 30.
8. St. Thomas Aquinas, *Summa*, vol. 5, pt. 3, q. 75, a. 4.
9. Council of Trent (1551): DS 1651.
10. Pope Paul VI, *Mysterium Fidei*, par. 52.
11. Joan Carroll Cruz, *Eucharistic Miracles* (Rockford, Ill.: TAN, 1987), 5–7.
12. *Catechism*, #1128.
13. St. Catherine of Siena, *The Dialogue*, ch. 110, 207.
14. Garrigou-Lagrange, vol. 1, 418.
15. Garrigou-Lagrange, vol. 1, 419.
16. Canon Jacques Leclercq, *The Interior Life*, trans. Fergus Murphy (New York: P.J. Kenedy & Sons, 1961), 88.

17. James T. O'Connor, *The Hidden Manna: A Theology of the Eucharist* (San Francisco: Ignatius, 1988), 322.
18. Ronald Lawlor, O.F.M., Cap., "Ordinary Faith in the Eucharist," *Catholic Dossier*, no. 5 (Sept.–Oct. 1996), 28.
19. Pope John Paul II, *Apostolic Letter on the Mystery and Worship of the Holy Eucharist*, no. 3.
20. Fulton J. Sheen, *Treasure in Clay: The Autobiography of Fulton J. Sheen* (Garden City, N.Y.: Doubleday, Image Books, 1982), 194.
21. Ronda De Sola Chervin, *Prayers of the Women Mystics* (Ann Arbor, Mich.: Servant, 1992), 237.
22. Sister Faustina Kowalska, *The Diary of Sister M. Faustina Kowalska* (Stockbridge, Mass.: Marian, 1987), #483, #908, #1392.
23. Cruz, 198.
24. Benedict Groeschel, C.F.R. and James Monti, *In the Presence of Our Lord* (Huntington, Ind.: Our Sunday Visitor, 1997), 81–82.
25. Groeschel and Monti, 82.
26. *St. Joseph "Continuous" Sunday Missal* (New York: Catholic Book, 1958–1957), 1256.

SEVEN
Resurrection: Made New for the Abundant Life

1. Cf. Col 1:24-25; 2 Cor 12:7-10; *Catechism of the Catholic Church*, #1508, #1521.
2. Frank Minirth, M.D., and Paul Meier, M.D., *Happiness Is a Choice* (Grand Rapids, Mich.: Baker, 1994), 106.
3. Consider this excerpt taken from *Happiness Is a Choice*, 112–13:

    The pituitary gland.... releases such hormones as ACTH (adrenocorticotropic hormone), growth hormone, luteinizing hormone, prolactin, and thyroid stimulating hormone.... The pituitary gland is actually controlled by the nearby hypothalamus.... The hypothalamus secretes releasing factors, which cause the pituitary to release the above-mentioned hormones. It is further known that these releasing factors from the hypothalamus are controlled by biogenic amines such as norepinephrine. Of course, this is a chemical, along with serotonin, that is known to be depleted in cases of depression. Thus, if there is a disturbance in the biogenic amines in the brain, depression results, and there also may be an endocrine abnormality. This has indeed been proven to be the case. It has been found that in cases of depression there is an elevation of cortisol (stress hormone) levels in the blood. One possible scenario is as follows. When cortisol levels are increased, lymphocytes (certain white blood cells) are suppressed. Lymphocytes produce antibodies. With *fewer antibodies*, the individual becomes more susceptible to nearly all physical illnesses. In other words, pent-up anger results in decreased norepinephrine, which results in increased ACTH releasing factor from the hypothalamus, which results in increased ACTH from the pituitary gland, which results in increased cortisol release from the adrenal gland (near the kidneys), which results in decreased lymphocytes, which results in decreased antibodies, which results in susceptibility to nearly all infectious diseases. *Pent-up anger is probably the leading cause of death.*

4. Six steps of forgiveness, identified by Dr. David Stoop, *Forgiving Our Parents, Forgiving Ourselves* (Ann Arbor, Mich.: Servant, 1991), 169–79:
    1. *Recognize the injury* - admit our anger.
    2. *Identify the emotions involved* – three emotions usually predominate: fear, shame, and anger.

3. *Express our hurt and anger* – talk them out with a friend or write them out in our journal.
4. *Set boundaries* – remove ourselves from harmful situations or relationships.
5. *Cancel the debt* – make a decision to forgive and do it.
6. *Consider reconciliation* – the ideal outcome of forgiveness but it is not always possible because all parties concerned must agree to it.
5. Cf. 1 Cor 12:8.

EIGHT
Carrying Out the Mission: Embracing the Abundant Life

1. Pope John Paul II, *On the Dignity and Vocation of Women*, par. 30.
2. Closing Speeches, 29.
3. Vatican Council II, *Lumen Gentium*, par. 62.
4. Thomas Aquinas, *Summa*, III, q. 26, art. 1.
5. Mark Miravalle, *Introduction to Mary* (Santa Barbara, Calif.: Queenship, 1993), 62.
6. Pope Paul VI, *Ad diem illum Laetissimum*, quoted by Miravalle, *Introduction to Mary*, 63.
7. Pope John Paul II, Homily in Granada, November 15, 1982.
8. St. Gregory the Great, *Homilies on the Gospels*, 19, 2.
9. Second Vatican Council, *Apostolicam actuositatem*, 12.
10. Pope John Paul II, *Mother of the Redeemer*, par. 47.
11. *Lumen Gentium* par. 62.
12. *Lumen Gentium*, par. 60.
13. Mark Miravalle, *Mary: Coredemptrix, Mediatrix, Advocate* (Santa Barbara, Calif.: Queenship, 1993), 61.
14. *Lumen Gentium*, par. 62.
15. Ronda De Sola Chervin, *Quotable Saints* (Ann Arbor, Mich.: Servant, 1992), 192.
16. Fernandez, *In Conversation with God*, vol. 3, 91.2, 592. Italics are quoting Pius XI, *Casti connubii*, 31, Dec. 1930.
17. Josemaría Escrivá, par. 831, 285.
18. Miravalle, *Introduction to Mary*, 70–72.
19. *The Navarre Bible, The Gospel of Luke* (Dublin: Colour Books, 1988), 59.
20. *Lumen Gentium*, par. 61–62.
21. Josemaría Escrivá, *Christ Is Passing By* (Princeton, N.J.: Scepter, 1973), par. 101, 231–32.
22. Caryl Houselander, *The Risen Christ* (New York: Sheed and Ward, 1958), 10.
23. St. Thérèse of Lisieux, *The Autobiography of St. Thérèse of Lisieux, The Story of a Soul*, trans. John Beevers (New York: Doubleday, Image Books, 1957), ch. 7, 91.
24. St. Thérèse of Lisieux, *VIII Letter to Her Sister Celine*, quoted in *Thoughts of Saint Thérèse*, 141–42.
25. Stein, "Principles of Women's Education," from *The Collected Works of Edith Stein*, vol. 2, 119.